Devil Child

For "Reya," "Kayleigh," "Clara," "Raven," KV," and "Cendall,"
who took care of me when I needed it the most

1

Chapters

Content Warning

This book handles sensitive topics such as suicide, eating disorders, self-harm, gender dysphoria, and trauma. Please proceed reading with caution.

National Suicide Hotline: 988

Trevor Project LGBTQ+ Helpline: (866) 488-7386

Prologue

"The Lord rebuke you, Satan, and all of your demons and all of your imps who come parading before us. That's right, I called you demons and imps, who come and parade before us and pretend that you are part of this world."

-Florida Republican Representative, Webster Barnaby, regarding transgender individuals

We all watch the same sun rise in the East and set in the West. We base our days around it, waiting for a star to illuminate our world before beginning the mundane tasks of life. We ignore the morning dew settling on the grass, leaves, flowers, and weeds. We listen to rhythmical notes forming chords and melodies to amplify our moods. We close our ears to the noise surrounding us if it doesn't serve a purpose. We stare at screens for hours on end searching for a way to rest while having the entire world at our fingertips.

Our lives aren't entirely different and yet no life is synonymous with another. No two people have the same story despite the abundance of shared experiences. In the modern world, we have more insight into other people's lives than ever before and still there are human experiences left practically untouched by the general public. Nobody possesses the power to reach into another's mind; maybe life would be easier if humans had developed such a skill.

Misunderstanding is the humble beginning of hatred.

My name is Faber Elliott Laurence, I'm seventeen years old and a transgender boy. For fifteen years of my life, I lived as a girl. I had long straight blonde hair that was silky and soft to the touch. I tried my hardest to fit into the box of girlhood I was expected to gracefully adapt to. I always knew I was different; I didn't have the vocabulary to express it, so I remained quiet. Not being able to understand myself fully gave me the desire to understand everyone else around me. The walls of silence I built around myself pushed me to peer out of windows to avoid staring at the opaque plaster. As I observed others and connected with them, I noticed that many people surrounding me seemed closed off to people they perceived as different. Even my own family was guilty of this form of judgement, and I didn't quite understand why.

Now I am the person who is perceived as different. Unfortunately, many people didn't spend the majority of their lives observing people through windows as I did and are content to spend their days encased in plaster. This is why it is important to me to share my story.

Chapter One: It's a Boy

"Transgenderism must be eradicated from public life entirely — the whole preposterous ideology, at every level."

-Michael Knowles

The first time I fully realized I was a boy was December 30, 2021. During the past few months, my head had grown louder and louder, screaming in sorrow and desperation. The weight I was feeling didn't even lift during my birthday a few weeks prior and I had cried nearly the entire day. I spent a lot of my days crying back then, puffy eyes and a reddened nose had become a signature look of mine. Every night after I showered, I laid on the bathroom floor and cradled myself as I cried in the unlit bathroom.

I had already accepted that my identity fell under the transgender umbrella, but I had identified as gender queer for the past year. I had been binding my chest for six months by that time and had begged my mom for a "Leonardo DiCaprio haircut" for a year to no avail. I had already changed my name to Faber and went by that name everywhere besides my own home. I was able to convince my parents to allow me to get my hair cut so that it reached the middle of my neck rather than my waist, but it hardly helped as I was still perceived as a girl. Even I saw a girl when I looked into the mirror, perhaps the most disappointing realization that each day brought.

I tried to make the best of the situation. I wore mascara and eyeliner in an attempt to find a sense of belonging with the other girls. I was used to this self-denial, a year prior to accepting that I wasn't a girl, I forced myself to wear pink and makeup and do all the feminine things I hated to try to force myself into conformity. I was no longer trying to force myself to be a girl, only to at least fit in with them. Though I exclusively wore masculine clothes and binded my chest flat, from the neck up I looked like a girl and was unable to change it so instead I hesitantly accepted it.

Late that December night, my mind became louder than it ever had been before. The nagging feeling of dysphoria broke through the noise screaming, "Don't you understand that you're a boy? Why can't you listen to me? Why can't you understand?" I realized the reason I cried after every shower stemmed from the betrayal of my own body. The reason I couldn't find happiness in life was because I was trapped in the wrong body and I couldn't bring myself to accept who I was. I wasn't just "not a girl," I was a boy.

I remember the mascara making shaky trails down my face that night as I cried. I knew my family would never understand, I knew I was condemned to live in this cage of a body until I was an independent adult, I knew the sadness wouldn't stop. In that moment, it was a helpless realization. Everything finally made sense, but I couldn't fix the problem.

That night, I printed a bunch of pictures representing the boyhood my heart, soul, and brain longed for. A cake exclaiming "It's a Boy," a suit and tie, a boy on a skateboard. I pasted them onto a paper in a brown leather journal, forming a collage. As I cried over the depiction of boyhood, I knew I was done denying myself. I was ready to fight for the life I deserved, a life as a boy.

In my sorrow, I hurt myself. I had been self-harming daily for the past year already, I made three rugged slices on my forearm. I cut a sock into a partial sleeve and slid it onto my arm to absorb the blood. The fabric of the sock was quickly soaked in blood, but it didn't transfer onto the sleeve of the hoodie I wore to bed. I wiped off the makeup staining my face, turned off the lights, and fell asleep with my cheek laying in the cool puddle of tears collecting on my pillow.

I continued to cry after every shower. I learned not to look down at my body and to turn off the lights. I came out quickly to my closest friends who I knew would accept me, most of whom already knew and were waiting for me to figure myself out. My house remained the only place I wasn't treated as a boy, which made it the humble home of my depression and dysphoria. My parents had made their stance on transgender people abundantly clear, they believed they were sick and confused.

Despite this, I came out to my parents less than a month after my realization. Being a boy felt so right, I knew I would never change so I saw no point in waiting to come out. I never came out to my parents as gender queer because somewhere deep down I knew it wasn't truly me, this was different. I needed my parents' help. I was tired of crying after every shower, of being trapped in my body, it was time for medical intervention. I texted my mother while my parents were out of the house to avoid the immediate backlash stating, "Mom, I'm trans and I want to go on puberty blockers." I feared I was already too far along into puberty for hormone blockers to have a significant effect, but I knew I had a better chance of accessing them than testosterone.

At first, no response came. I waited anxiously in my room, texting my friend Belle to distract me from the chaos that was inevitably to come. The response from my parents was as I expected it to be, a hard, set in stone no. My father asked me questions regarding why I wanted to be a boy and informed me that I could do boy activities whilst still being a girl. I knew that of course, but I wasn't a girl, I was a boy. He insisted that God made me to be a girl, I didn't believe in his God.

I had come so far, realizing who I was alone had taken years to fully accept. I had finally figured out why none of the puzzle pieces of my life seemed willing to conjoin into a cohesive piece. My parents' reaction informed me that it was all for nothing. A familiar feeling crept over me once more, the urge to disappear entirely, to instantly end this twisted game I was forced to play that everyone referred to as life. I didn't necessarily want to die, rather to simply cease existing. But if death is what it took, is that such a high price to pay?

Chapter Two: Devil Child

"We worry about what a child will become tomorrow, yet we forget that he is someone today."

-Stacia Tauscher

I was born a girl, with an entirely different name, on December 7, 2005, in Ohio. I was my parents' first child and as such I received their undivided attention during my first years of life. My parents said I was a well-behaved baby, hardly crying and following directions from a young age. My father was employed for a large company and my mother worked as a therapist for court mandated sex offenders. Their work schedules occasionally conflicted and I was babysat by my mother's friend during those times. By two or three, I was enrolled in a preschool and began to learn how to make friends and socialize with other children.

A month after I had turned three, my brother was born. My parents named him Aidan Eugene, with his middle name being a family name passed down by my father's side of the family for generations. He was my polar opposite, loud, rambunctious, and needy from the time he was born. He constantly caused chaos, spilling milk purposely, scratching windows and chairs with sandpaper, throwing dramatic temper tantrums, and occasionally becoming violent. He received many timeouts and spankings, and singlehandedly turned our quiet house into a loud environment. Nonetheless, he had a gentle side to him, and I spent my time playing with him and doting over him.

When my brother and I misbehaved as young children, our father would call us "Devil Child." My mother hated this phrase, especially when I began drawing pictures in elementary school of my brother with horns labeled "Devil Child." This only happened in front of my parents once, when I was drawing a picture to place inside of a clear cup. They reprimanded me, telling me it wasn't funny. Seeing as my brother was most often given the nickname, I heavily associated him with it and didn't understand their reaction.

I was labeled a gifted child as soon as I entered kindergarten. I was miles ahead of the other children academically and never stumbled when introduced to new concepts. My teacher showed me off to the principal and often complemented my reading abilities. I enjoyed school and was excited to learn every day. Teachers began to fight over me and by first grade, I was doing both first and second grade work simultaneously. I enjoyed being in my own reading group, reading chapter books instead of picture books. Occasionally, my teacher would give me Mentos as a treat for working so hard independently.

I began creating stories before I could even write, telling them to my father as he typed them up on the family computer for me and printed them out. They often revolved around the lives of my stuffed animals or orphaned children. As I began to write independently, my teachers were often concerned by the dark tones of my stories, but I quite enjoyed desolate tales. The characters in my books almost never had parents and if they did, they died early in the plotline. Even my relatives discouraged me from writing such melancholy plots and eventually my writing became a topic of secrecy.

At home, my father always had always possessed a burning temper. When we received spankings, he would send us up to our rooms to wait until he could calm down enough to discipline us appropriately. The time spent waiting was torturous, we would cry alone until we heard footsteps ascending the stairs and began to wail harder. Sometimes, when our mother was at work, my father would lie in his bed unresponsive, and I was forced to care for my brother. We would yell at him to wake up, jump on his bed, turn on the lights, to no avail.

I was mature and always ready to fix my brother a slice of buttered bread and tuck him into bed. I remember my brother coming to get me while I was in the bath, telling me that "Daddy is asleep again." I drained the water, got dressed, put my hair into a ponytail, and watched over him for the rest of the evening. I was likely around seven. I didn't mind it very much at the time, I found it fun to play the role of a parent and I've always possessed an empathetic and gentle demeanor as well as a love for children.

On one occasion, my brother and I were searching for a green stuffed crab we had lost. We formed a miniature search party and looked throughout the entire house. When I opened the access door to the pipes in our herbal green painted bathroom, I found some unopened bottles resting inside. I ran to my mother to show her what I believed the old owners of the house had left behind and asked her if I could drink the one labeled "Hard Lemonade." She seemed quite flustered and refused my request while taking the bottles away from me, insisting that she knew exactly who had left them there. My father never hid alcohol there again, but it wasn't long before I figured out what I had actually stumbled upon.

From the time I was four, I had been enrolled in gymnastics. I wasn't particularly gifted in the sport, but I had a natural flexibility and a love for the sport. My father had been a gymnast as a child and likely hoped I would become as talented as he once was. By the time I was seven, I was spending twelve hours a week in the gym, climbing ropes, running around, swinging on bars, and learning how to do back handsprings. My coach, Philip, was an old man from Romania and was extremely strict and stern. He would sit on us while we were in our splits if we weren't all the way down. He had a soft spot for me, and often carried me around, asking if I would like to stay after practice. My mother was always uncomfortable with him and pulled me from his gym when I was eight.

By third grade, I began to resent being gifted. I was placed with a new teacher, who didn't know how to handle my abilities. She put me on an online learning regimen and never provided me with the books the other kids sat on the rug and worked on with her. While they discussed, and read, and worked together, I sat in a corner using one of the communal computers watching videos teaching me concepts far beyond my grade level. I struggled through the homework she only gave to me, as I've never learned well online. I began to cry over my work at home and insist that I didn't understand what I had never formally been taught.

My teacher recommended to my parents that I should talk to a therapist after I began rubbing my hands on the rug aggressively to give

11

myself bleeding rugburns. I enjoyed the stinging pain and the droplets of blood that formed. It didn't seem much different to me than trying to break my bones which I had been doing since first grade by hammering my wrists on metal basketball hoop poles, hitting myself repeatedly with hard objects when I was alone, or trying to twist my ankles as I walked. My parents didn't take me to see a therapist and the behavior continued.

Seeing that I had been entirely separated from the rest of my class, the teacher decided to start sending me up to a fourth-grade classroom for half of the school day. I looked forward to that portion of my day as I was finally able to talk to other students and collaborate on work. I quickly made friends with the fourth graders and grew attached to the teacher. I was allowed to read the same books as the other kids and do the same activities, I hardly even touched a computer. While I struggled to enjoy the atmosphere of my own classroom, the fourth-grade classroom enabled me to fall in love with school again and I continued to excel. I had tested at a college reading level from the time I was in first grade, and I still wasn't particularly challenged, but I was being actively taught and had created a community of fellow students.

During that year, I began to have weeks in a row where I ate very little and lost weight rapidly, claiming that I felt sick. I started missing a lot of school and becoming a frequent visitor to the school nurse. I was prescribed a medication that helped a bit and began to have fewer episodes. I had a phobia of throwing up and was absolutely paralyzed by the idea of it, which made the whole situation worse and discouraged me from eating. I started refusing to go to gymnastics when I wasn't feeling well and often cried in the bathroom when I did go to practice. Nobody knew exactly what was going on, but I was later diagnosed with severe anxiety and panic attacks.

I also remember my first experience of dysphoria occurring when I was around nine years old. Before going to gymnastics, I snuck into my mother's closet and found her bra stuffers. I placed them inside of my leotard, expecting to love the results as I was supposed to be excited about growing up. I looked in the mirror and was overcome by a strong sense of disgust. It looked so wrong and alien to me, I hated everything about it. I quickly removed the bra stuffers and placed them back in the closet, grateful that I didn't have breasts yet.

By fourth grade, I began receiving awards from the school board for my achievements in school. Accolades for my reading, writing, math, and drawing abilities were presented to me during school board meetings. I had been taught not to brag so I remained relatively humble about it all, but it only reinforced my perfectionistic tendencies towards school. I had been presented with an award at the school assemblies every year of elementary school prior as I impressed all of my teachers, but these acknowledgements were greater and more valuable to me.

In Ohio, the last year of elementary school is fourth grade with fifth and sixth grade being middle school and seventh and eighth grade belonging to junior high. I was invited to an invite only gifted program hosted at the local junior high school for my fifth through eighth grade years. I eagerly accepted but grew to regret my decision after learning that all my close friends were attending an entirely different school, and I was the only one who had been invited into the Gateway program. My parents informed me that it was too late to change my mind, and I entered the junior high school entirely alone on my first day of fifth grade.

The school was much larger than my previous school and as I walked upstairs to find my locker for the first time, I was intimidated by the older kids. I've always been short for my age, and they towered above me. I quickly found my locker and was pleased to see that all the fifth graders' lockers were next to each other and the kids turning combination locks around me seemed just as nervous. I saw a familiar face, a girl from my school named Annaliese and asked if we could walk to class together. We had all the same classes and quickly became best friends, adding a girl named Violet to our friend group somewhere along the way.

The gifted program was a place of solace for me. Nobody there was "normal." One of my teachers had OCD and occasionally made bird noises during class, another played with putty while teaching

13

as a way to cope with her anxiety. The students there were diverse as well and I didn't feel out of place like I had in the past. While I still wasn't entirely challenged by the work, I was finally on the same level as everyone else. I was able to collaborate with people and discuss assignments. I was even able to join the writing club, becoming the youngest member.

The downside of the gifted program was that we were expected to grow up quickly. While the other middle schoolers still got recess, we no longer had one as we ran on the same schedule as the junior high students. Occasionally, the teachers would take us outside to throw a ball around to make up for our lack of recess. The gesture was always appreciated, and our little crew of misfits would play blissfully. We were expected to have longer attention spans than the average fifth graders but were allowed to use fidget toys to aid us. I kept a pocket of my backpack stocked with miscellaneous fidget toys to aid me in my endeavor to focus for the never-ending cycle of class periods.

A group of the most popular fifth grade girls quickly banded together, calling themselves The Savage Patch Kids. Annaliese, Violet, and I found them annoying and stuck up. We tried to ignore them for the most part, but occasionally whispered snide remarks about them. Our little group was artistic and creative, and we often hung out together in the library, bathroom, or under the bleachers during gym. We took pictures on Annaleise's red digital camera often, documenting the adventures we went on inside the school walls.

In late fall of that year, a school dance was hosted at the school my elementary friends attended and I decided to go. The school they went to looked odd to me and we hardly danced. At some point during the dance, I told them about how my dad's temper had gotten worse at home. My brother's temper tantrums had increased, and the amount of fighting had increased along with it.

The next day, I was called into the guidance counselors office. It was a dim office and had a calm atmosphere. The counselor, Ms. Kyte, asked, "Does your father ever hit you?"

I knew to tell the truth, "Yes."

"With a closed hand or open hand?" She demonstrated a fist in one hand and a flat palm in the other.

I also knew this was not the time to exaggerate anything, "Only with an open hand."

She nodded, "Does this happen to both you and your brother?"

"Mostly my brother, he doesn't behave very well. It only happens to me when I'm bad and I'm not really a bad kid."

"Where does he hit you?" she prompted, writing things down in a small notepad.

"Usually, he pulls our pants down and spanks us but sometimes he'll grab our arms or something instead," I explained nervously.

"And does your mom know about this?" she asked.

"Yeah, she knows. He just gets angry sometimes and it's mostly my brother anyways," I bargained.

"You and your brother's stories line up," she remarked. My brother was seven at the time attending second grade at the elementary school, I was surprised this had been traced back to him as well. "You can go back to lunch now."

I walked back into the lunchroom confused and shaky. I didn't understand why I had been talked to or what would happen, so I continued throughout my day. I talked to my friends about the strange encounter, and we discussed how invasive the line of questioning was. Everyone gets mad on occasion, and spankings were a common practice, so I assumed nothing would come of it. I was wrong.

When my mom picked me up from school, she was scathing. "You got dad reported to CPS!"

"What?" I exclaimed. "I didn't do anything! I just told the truth!"

"Yeah, well one of you told them that dad hits you, and grabs you, and pushes you, and kicks you! If he was really that bad, I would've divorced him! Is that what you want?" The only part of that statement that I didn't know about was the kicking. Aiden must have said it, but I wasn't sure if it was true, perhaps it had been done in private.

"No! I don't want you to divorce. I'm sorry, I really didn't mean to do anything," I pleaded.

Before going to gymnastics that evening, where my father worked as an assistant coach to pay for my lessons, I decided to interrogate Aiden. I took him into the spare bedroom in our house and sat him down on the tiny bed. "Aiden, when they talked to you today, did you tell them that dad kicked you?"

"Yes," he admitted through the gaps in his teeth. "My teacher said they were reporting him."

"So it was really your story that got him reported?" I accused.

"Yeah, right after I talked to them, they said they were reporting him," he shared nonchalantly. He had no idea what was going on and I was the one absorbing all the anger from my mother. It really wasn't my fault; my accusations alone wouldn't have gotten him reported.

I went to gymnastics that night with a depressed attitude. I didn't understand entirely what was going on either, I was only ten and I feared my father would be going to jail. I told my friends about my fears but forced them to promise they wouldn't tell their parents. Of course, they did, and when my mom came to pick me up, she was surrounded by parents asking her questions. It was clear that I had messed up again, but I didn't understand what I had done wrong.

When I got into the car with my mother, she began to berate me about how my dad wouldn't be able to work at the gym anymore

16

and asked me if I was trying to ruin his life. I wasn't trying to ruin his life, as far as I knew, everything I had said had been true. I began to cry, over the pressure being placed on me. I felt like a terrible, terrible child. I couldn't do anything right. I *was* a Devil Child. Whoever had told the school counselor about my dad had ruined my life and in return, I had ruined his.

Besides crying over it several more times and constantly being reminded of what I had done by my parents, nothing else came of the report. My dad was far more careful though, and the arguments between him and my brother dissolved into being exclusively verbal. My brother was never reprimanded for the situation and never admitted to my parents that it wasn't my fault so I continued to take the blame. I became a slightly more wounded version of myself, staying quiet in school, gymnastics, and home.

A few months after the report, my dad announced that we were moving due to his job relocating him. We were moving to a town called Normal, Illinois. I found the name of it entertaining; it was such a peculiar name for a town. It was six hours away from where we lived at the time, and it meant that I would have to leave the only house I had ever known. We began to renovate our humble beige house in preparation to sell it and hosting open houses. I enjoyed the open houses as it meant my brother and I got to go shopping until the time period had ended.   My brother's birthday, which is in the middle of winter, came around and we still hadn't moved. We had a joint birthday party at the arcade near our house to celebrate. We began traveling to Illinois to find a house soon after the party. Our realtor's car was filled with the pungent scent of cigarettes, and I coughed violently when he exited the car. I wrote down notes on each house in a burgundy notebook as we walked through them. All of the houses were double the size of the one we currently resided in, and I was in awe of their structure and beauty.

Finally, we settled on a house and sold our own. In February, my brother and I lived with our grandparents for a week while my parents moved everything into the new house. When our stay with our grandparents ended, we drove to the novel white house with dark teal shutters. Stepping inside of it was surreal, it still felt sterile and not yet like a home. We ran upstairs to pet our beloved guinea pig, Butterscotch, and explore our new rooms. Mine had been painted lilac and had the theme of Paris while my brother's remained beige with a nautical theme.

I was driven to gymnastics and quickly made new friends both there and at school. Fifth grade was still considered elementary school age in Illinois, and I was placed back into an elementary school. There were no gifted programs, and my test scores quickly singled me out again. Despite working on different projects than my classmates and often residing in the corridor rather than the classroom, everyone wanted to be my friend since I was the new kid. With only a few months left until I graduated elementary school for the second time, I didn't struggle as much with the isolation as I had in previous years.

Moving to Illinois didn't come without a bit of hardship. My mother wasn't yet licensed to work in Illinois and became a stay-at-home mom temporarily while she worked towards earning her new licensure. Becoming a single income family suddenly as well as moving into a far more expensive house than our previous one put a financial strain on the family. Besides gymnastics, the activities we participated in had to be free. It was a summer filled with parks and fishing trips, which quickly bored me as I've never been particularly fond of spending extended periods of time outdoors.

That summer, my gym was bought out by another gym and the two establishments combined. The new owners, Drake and Esme, were strict and mean and brought out the worst of my anxiety. I was training to compete in level six but became so anxious that I decided to stay in level four for another year. My biggest fear was jumping to catch the high bar. It was so far away, and I couldn't reach it easily with my short frame. They attempted to punish me into conquering my fear, forcing me to repeatedly climb ropes that reached the ceiling until my feet were raw and bleeding and leaving me entirely alone at the bars while the other kids moved on to a different event.

Even still, I was afraid and hardly ever caught the bar. One day, I jumped to catch the bar and missed it once more. My ankle twisted on the edge of the mat and I fell into an awkward heap. A sharp pain forced tears into my eyes and I began to sob. A nicer coach, Ken, carried me to off to the side and laid me on the ground while he instructed a girl to get ice for me. The ice stung and I continued to sob for half an hour. Once I was able to stop crying, my ankle was numb and red and had swollen up to the size of a golf ball. It looked disgusting and visibly deformed but the coaches had moved on and I was lying alone.

I heard Drake snicker from behind me, "Hey, did you break your ankle by catching the high bar or not catching it?"

"Not catching it," I sniffled.

"Lesson learned, no more crying over it. Just catch it next time," he jeered.

I wish anxiety were that easy to conquer.

I was given weights to lift as I stared at the ceiling for the remaining three hours of practice and was eventually carried onto the floor to perform one-legged push-ups. Injured or not, strength was still a priority in gymnastics. They failed to call my mom and when she came to pick me up, she was surprised to see me hopping towards her on one foot. I went to the hospital and got a purple cast, but not before the horrific bruise had spread up my calf and down to my toes.

Chapter Three: House of Skeletons

"Conformity is the jailer of freedom and the enemy of growth."

-John F. Kennedy

I began my sixth-grade year on crutches, having finally quit the only sport I had ever known. I wasn't afraid of beginning junior high again, I had felt extremely out of place at elementary school. At this point in my life, I was at the peak of my academic abilities and still possessed the energy and motivation to conquer any work thrown at me. I was placed in an advanced math class, two years ahead of my grade level. No other classes offered advanced placements, which was a bit disappointing, but I decided I would just fly through them.

A few weeks into school, I got my cast removed only to find that my ankle hadn't properly healed yet and was still painful. They placed a second cast on me, with the instructions to attempt to walk on it using a special shoe on top of the cast. I found it extremely painful and stuck to the crutches for the most part until the following appointment when I was given a boot. By this point, I had been on crutches for over two months, and everyone was confused as to why I was still in pain. The doctors told my mom it was likely due to anxiety and sent me on my way.

We had a family trip to Disney World in October that year. I was still unable to walk independently so I was confined to a wheelchair for the duration of the trip. It wasn't a terrible experience, I never got tired from walking, I got to skip the lines for rides, and the characters were even more friendly when they interacted with me than they typically were. At one point during the trip, my brother ate too much food and began throwing up when we got back to the hotel. My phobia of puke got the better of me and I hopped on one foot out the door of the hotel and down the streets of Disney with tears in my eyes. My dad had to run after me with my wheelchair and wheel me around the park until I agreed to go back into the hotel room. Nobody could have guessed how much that single experience would affect me.

A few weeks later, my brother joined the local swim team. Watching him swim gave me the motivation to attempt to walk on my own, despite the pain I felt. Once I was able to walk again, I joined the team as well eagerly. I was naturally better than my uncoordinated brother, and my age caused the coaches to push me harder as well. For a while, it was an enjoyable sport that I was able to do well in. Unfortunately, my body was slowly deteriorating and would soon cause me to leave the sport entirely.

At home, I began having problems eating. I was terrified of making the same mistake as my brother and eating to the point of being sick. I slowly decreased the amount of food I was able to eat without fearing being sick until the amount was minimal. I became obsessed with checking the dates of food to ensure it wasn't expired and wouldn't make me sick. I wouldn't eat anything unless I was able to check the expiration date first. I told my parents that something must be physically wrong with me when my doctors noticed a drop in my weight. I quit swimming as my body became tired extremely quickly and my weight continued to decline. At my lowest weight, my grandmother walked into me while I was naked and remarked that I looked like a starving prisoner from a concentration camp.

I was taken to a specialist who diagnosed me with Avoidant Restrictive Food Intake Disorder or ARFID, an eating disorder. I fought against this diagnosis; I wasn't trying to lose weight. The decisions I was making weren't intentional or done with the goal of dropping weight, I couldn't understand how that translated into an eating disorder. Regardless, I was dropping around two pounds a week, and was given a week to gain weight before I was hospitalized. The doctor provided me with Pediasure nutritional shakes in an attempt to help, but I refused to consume them.

A week later, I was hospitalized for the first time. I refused to eat anything by mouth the first night I was there. The following day, my bed was rolled into an ocean themed room after I had been given a sedative to calm me down. A nurse shoved a thin plastic tube, called an NG tube, up my nose. It went down my throat and into my stomach and a machine pumped Pediasure liquid through it. I was tube fed four times a day and put on a strict 6 meals a day meal plan on top of the tube feedings. I spent a lot of time crying from the stomach pain I faced.

I had an ankle bracelet installed to ensure I didn't leave the floor and my requests to go outside were ignored. I spent most of my time in the game room playing on the PlayStation 2 with a friend I made there named Noel. She was in the hospital to have gallbladder surgery and we were only able to play together for a few days before she was put on bedrest to recover from her surgery. I wasn't allowed to go home with the NG tube, so I had to focus on learning to eat and drink enough by mouth to sustain myself. After spending a week in the hospital with the NG tube, I was allowed to pull it out myself and was sent home.

The school year ended only a few days after I got home, and summer began. I became withdrawn and disinterested in doing anything, unable to process my hospital stay or my feelings around it. I was put into therapy, but I still refused to say I had an eating disorder, so it was largely unhelpful. I told my therapist I never wanted to grow up. I explained how I never wanted to wear makeup or dresses or fulfill the societal roles of a woman and not eating allowed me to remain in a child-like body. I was told I would never go through puberty if I didn't eat, a statement that would stick with me forever. Of course, my therapist had meant to motivate me by saying that, but it was heavily misguided.

I was forced to participate in summer theater despite having just returned from the hospital. I didn't want to go and protested against it. My mother insisted that I at least tried it, and I reluctantly agreed. On my first day there, I met a girl a year older than me named Bronwyn. She had long brown hair and was nearly a foot taller than me. She was beautiful and had the most incredible singing voice. After meeting her, I decided I liked theater camp after all and spent the rest of the summer following her around like a puppy. She went to a different school to me, and I was sad when theater camp ended and we returned to our separate universes.

During this time, my brother was slightly overweight, and my parents began restricting his food to ensure he wouldn't overeat. He would cry asking for snacks only to be denied. I started helping him because I was encouraged to eat as much as I wanted. I would grab food multiple times a day and put it in the drawers under his bed. He appreciated my help and often requested different items. I didn't believe my parents were doing the right thing by restricting his intake forcefully, so I didn't feel guilty lying to them about the food I took. He still received three meals a day and was by no means starved, but he was often still hungry after meals or in between them and wasn't allowed to eat more.

My brother also threw loud, dramatic temper tantrums almost daily. I couldn't call or FaceTime my friends because there would be screaming in the background every night. My dad would yell at him at the top of his lungs, escalating the situation. One time, my parents even called the police to embarrass him. I occasionally filmed the chaos to document how unbearable it had become. I would often try to talk to my brother calmly to relax him, but my dad would yell at me to stop being "the good guy" because it made him look bad. Home was a miserable place to be, a constant screaming match between my brother and my dad.

I spent a lot of my seventh-grade year under the threat of being taken to an eating disorder facility. My weight often fluctuated, and the doctor pressed my parents to admit me to a facility. I feared the idea, I didn't want to live in a house of sick kids, I imagined it to be like living in a house of skeletons. Besides, I wasn't sick in the same way they were, I wasn't intentionally starving myself, I was just afraid of eating too much and throwing up. My parents agreed that I was too young to be sent away from home for treatment and I spent my days crying at the family dinner table as I was pushed to eat. My parents finally motivated me by agreeing to let me get a pet hamster if I reached a certain weight.

I reached that weight shortly after my thirteenth birthday and got a light orange and white hamster I named Peanut. She was my pride and joy and I often spent hours decorating her cage into extravagantly themed displays. I had done mountains of research before buying her to ensure she had a properly sized enclosure and high-quality food and toys. After I got Peanut, I struggled a lot less with eating and for a while, things were calm. I was just like any other kid. I no longer had to follow a strict meal plan and I stopped crying at every meal.

Throughout all of junior high, I had begged to sing in the boy's section of choir. I genuinely didn't understand why I wasn't developing like all the other boys. Of course, I knew I was supposed to be a girl and I didn't vocally deny being a girl. I was extremely sheltered and wasn't even aware of the existence of transgender people yet. This caused a lot of confusion for me, and I was always attempting to fit in with or at the very least compete against boys. I crashed my brother's Nerf gun birthday party, forced myself to beat all of the boys in the pushup test at school, and detested any sort of fashion, makeup, or girly activities.

By eighth grade, I was asking to join the wrestling team, eager to continue my father's high school wrestling legacy. When he refused to allow me to join the team, claiming it was "a boy's sport," I decided to date a wrestler instead. All of my friends had gotten boyfriends by that point, and I figured it was the closest I could get to wrestling. A boy named Ian and I began dating after having only one conversation together a few hours prior.

Ian had two married mothers and it was my first time being exposed to LGBTQ people knowingly in real life. They were incredibly kind to me and let Ian and I wrestle for fun. He always beat me since I had no training and he had been on the team for years, but we were similar in size, so I didn't get hurt and it was still enjoyable for me. Ian was very controlling over my appearance, asking me to send him pictures of my outfits before school each day and encouraging me to dye my hair brown. I wasn't allowed to dye my hair and I still felt no connection to the clothes I wore so I was pretty disappointing to him in the beginning.

I quickly became overly feminine for him and for myself. I wanted to fit in, this time with the girls as it wasn't exactly working in my favor to fit in with boys, and I believed it was time to at least attempt to be fashionable and conventionally attractive. I thought that if I pushed myself hard enough, I could conform into the woman society wanted me to be. Overnight, I went from strongly protesting wearing makeup to asking to buy some and wearing any clothes that fit me to insisting that I looked best in pink and loved rompers. The shift was hardly even noticed by my parents, they thought it was just a normal part of my development. Nobody regarded it as anything special, but it was exhausting to me.

I became more active on social media and did everything in my power to paint myself as a pretty girl. It was all an act, the only thing I cared about was being perceived as pretty. I had almost no relationship with my inner self or my own thoughts or feelings, how I looked in the mirror each morning was all that mattered. I smeared mascara on my long lashes and patted blush on my cheeks. I brushed my long hair constantly, obsessing over it looking perfect and feeling silky. I began putting my hair into intricate styles, spending more time on it than I ever had before. Only a few years before, I had been teased for my childish style and my preference for covering up my hair with a hat. I had finally become the girl everyone expected me to be.

I joined archery in eighth grade as a sort of compromise to myself. My dad had become involved in it, and it made me feel masculine despite how feminine I looked. I was a natural at it and soon started competing in competitions. I never won any competitions as the other competitors had better equipment and were years ahead of me in experience. Still, it made me feel strong and set me apart from the other girls. I envied them, it seemed so natural for them to grow up and become women. I didn't understand why it was so hard for me, but I put in all my effort while doing small things like archery to satisfy myself.

I participated in a holiday musical and began taking voice lessons from one of the directors named Michael. He gave his students all of the solos in the show, and I figured taking lessons from him would give me a better chance of getting a solo the following year. I ended up hating the experience immensely and deciding not to go back, but I was nevertheless elated to finally begin receiving voice lessons. I had always wanted to sing with the boys in choir, but with this newfound obligation of femininity, I decided to work on highering my range rather than lowering it. It wasn't pleasant work, I had always had a lower range and felt like a fish out of water trying to squeal through high notes with little instruction from Michael aside from encouragement.

Following the sudden switch in my physical appearance and interests, we received the news that school would be shut down for the two weeks prior to spring break due to COVID 19. I had heard about the virus, my friends had described it as "the new plague." We had begun making jokes about it in class when someone coughed, but it hadn't seemed so funny when we had to listen to the long list of events that had been canceled over the loudspeakers. I personally had thought everyone was being incredibly dramatic and was embarrassed when my dad began making my brother and I wear gloves and masks to go to the grocery stores.

Soon after schools shut down, Ian and I broke up. He claimed he liked me better when I looked more plain and COVID was causing our relationship to feel as though it was long distance even though we lived in the same city. I was glad he called it off, I had just begun to come to the conclusion that I was attracted to girls, and I wasn't sure how I felt about boys. I had never liked kissing Ian and often pretended to be sick or secretly asked my mom to invade our space so he wouldn't have the chance to kiss me. Everything felt so odd and out of place, and I was ready to move on and figure things out for myself. Ian tried desperately to get back together with me after our breakup, but I turned him down.

After spring break, schools didn't reopen, and things changed rapidly. We were now forced to shelter in place, and I began taking the pandemic seriously. My brother and I weren't allowed to go to stores anymore or leave the house without a mask and gloves on. Everyone wore masks, it was like a scene from a dystopian movie. It no longer felt embarrassing to be cautious, instead it felt responsible. Days were long and boring, with nowhere to go and nothing to do. We hardly had to do any schoolwork as teachers weren't sure how to teach entirely over the internet. Similar circumstances had never occurred during my lifetime, everything was so dystopian.

My best friend from school, Belle, was no longer allowed to visit my house due to the pandemic. Restaurants began placing food in front of cars rather than seating people inside. Toilet paper was nowhere to be seen along with hand sanitizer. I learned how to sew masks to make ones that fit my small face. I spent most of my days drawing or building small metal figures from the kits I had bought before we had to shelter in place. The entire summer was spent indoors with only short walks to break up our days.

Nearly every person on Earth had been paralyzed by fear simultaneously.

Chapter Four: Skins

"Do I want to die from the inside out or the outside in?"

-Laurie Halse Anderson

When my freshman year of high school began, I was at the height of my efforts to be feminine. The pandemic was also reaching its peak and due to that, all classes were online until further notice. On my first day of school, I wore a white floral romper and brushed my silky golden hair until it laid perfectly. My hair nearly reached my waist by that point, and it trailed down my back in perfect straight lines. I didn't turn my computer camera on that day, but it was the effort that counted. I sat in my white desk chair attempting to retain information blasted from my computer for seven hours straight.

I had just finished my first day of school when I looked down and saw the unimaginable, I had started my period. I had never had a period before, and a wave of sickness came over me. I was disgusted by what my body was doing, I wanted it to stop. I had been educated about periods, I knew what they were and why they occurred. To me, it signified something that I had never wanted to happen, it was the mark of becoming a woman. I knew immediately that I had been right when I was twelve, I wasn't meant to be a woman. The façade of femininity I had built around myself came crashing down quietly within me. I decided to continue to force myself to be feminine on the outside, but to sabotage the inner workings of my body.

I stole a tampon from my mother's bathroom to make the period seem non-existent while I waited for my plan to work. *"You won't go through puberty if you don't eat."* I wasn't entirely sure, but I hoped there was a possibility I could stop my puberty from continuing to progress if I stopped eating even after reaching this milestone. I had dance in the evenings, that would help me burn any calories I consumed. I had to make this horrific mistake stop, no matter what it took. Looking feminine on the outside was one thing, but having a body that functions as a woman's body was out of my control, a betrayal. Luckily, I knew how to regain the control I felt I had lost.

My favorite show at the time was Skins UK and I turned to it for advice. One of the characters, Cassie, struggled with an eating disorder and often discussed the tactics she used to maintain her disorder openly on the show. I watched clips of her on YouTube, analyzing every behavior she engaged in and memorizing them for my own use later. It was enlightening and enjoyable, like learning a new hobby. I saw no consequences in the near future at the time. After all, Cassie lived throughout the entire show and never had any lasting complications from refusing to eat.

And so, my real-life rendition of the Hunger Games began. I tracked every calorie I ate and burned on an app on my phone. I slowly reduced the amount I ate, beginning with smaller portions before eliminating meals entirely. I would show up to dance after an entire day of not eating and my dance coach would tell me I had "that look in my eyes." The look, as she explained, was a telltale sign that I hadn't eaten. I didn't understand what she meant at the time, I failed to see the hollow emptiness in my eyes as they looked desperately for sustenance.

I decided to come out to my parents as a lesbian in the beginning of my freshman year. It had taken me a while to accept that I couldn't just stop loving who I loved because it was seen as a sin. Once I finally came to terms with the idea that some "sins" weren't a choice, it was obvious to me that I was LGBTQ. There was no doubt in my mind that I liked women and I felt identifying as a lesbian was the closest I could get to being a boy. Coming out unleashed the worst sides of my parents as they struggled to even attempt to understand me. My relationship with them grew strained quickly as they broke my heart time and time again with their words and actions.

I turned to online forums to find people who understood me, it wasn't difficult since everything was online during that time. I met a woman named Cassie who claimed to be a French model and was also a lesbian. She told me she was 29 years old, and Cassie was only an internet name to conceal her true famous identity. We quickly became friends, and she complimented me frequently, telling me she thought I was twenty from my picture despite me only being fourteen at the time and certainly looking no older.

I also began talking to a girl named Lydia, a sixteen-year-old lesbian from Nevada. Lydia was a great online friend, she replied quickly and soon we had even exchanged numbers and our social medias. She struggled severely with mental health, however, and introduced me to a realm I had never ventured into before. She had a history of self-harming and would tell me how and when she did it. I often tried to prevent her from harming herself, but it was an impossible task. She would spiral into darkness and take me down with her, and soon I began following in her path.

It started out small, I would scratch myself just enough to draw some blood and create a shallow scab. My parents would usually notice and accuse me of cutting myself, I was telling the truth when I denied it. It quickly wasn't enough for me, and I began seeking new ways to release my emotions through pain. I saw a YouTube video of two boys who got third degree burns from putting ice and salt to their flesh and decided to try it. I put a small mountain of salt on my calf and pressed an ice cube into it. At first it provided me with sharp, satisfying stings, just reaching the border of unbearable pain. Quickly, all sensation left the area and I lifted the ice off to reveal a white, leathery patch of skin that was frozen solid in the most literal sense. I repeated my actions a couple more times a few inches apart from each other before I was content and able to stop myself.

The next day, the patches were red and swollen, looking similar to a localized allergic reaction. I wore long pants to school and leggings to dance to hide the area. As the days passed, the patches got progressively worse, first blistering and peeling, then scabbing nastily and becoming deeper as my pants stuck to the scabs and ripped them away from the wounds. I began to bandage them in an attempt to slow down the damage. While I was wrapping the bandage around my leg, my dad opened the bathroom door, and my secret was exposed.

He took me to the ER as my leg was looking quite grotesque. I was not pleased to be there and attempted to talk my way out of it, insisting to several doctors that I was fine. When asked why I did it, I played dumb. I told the doctors I had fallen for an internet challenge out of stupidity and had never intended to hurt myself. They believed my story and sent me home without a psychiatric evaluation, warning me that the patches would likely leave scars. Of course, I didn't mind this. In my mind, scars were proof that I was struggling, a twisted form of validation.

As I spiraled into darkness, Lydia did too. Soon she began telling me she was going to kill herself and I would spend hours glued to my phone talking her down from it. The first time it happened, I shook uncontrollably and cried. I hadn't felt as though talking to her constantly was important beforehand, but after she told me that I was the only thing she felt was worth living for, talking to her became a matter of life and death. Eventually, she asked me to be her girlfriend and I agreed. I had a crush on a few other girls from my school, but it didn't seem like Lydia was in a place to handle rejection. In the beginning, it was comforting to be able to say that I had a girlfriend, and I didn't mind that I truly only saw her as a friend.

It was a long-distance relationship, and I knew we wouldn't meet in person any time soon so the gap between friendship and dating was only a matter of words. We sent each other letters and packages, caring about each other like any normal couple our age. The abnormal part of our relationship lied in that we also cared *for* each other, mostly I cared for her. I smoothly transitioned into cutting myself after my ER visit, taking inspiration from Lydia. I was vague about my struggles to her, but as I continued to talk her down from suicide on a regular basis, I simultaneously struggled in a much quieter fashion.

I started cutting on my upper thigh, a part of me that was always covered to ensure nobody would find out about it. The costumes from dance often threatened to reveal my secret to my parents, but I always found a way to cover it up, be it physically or through excuses. The girls in my dance class and my coach were aware of my self-mutilation but stayed relatively quiet about it. On occasion, I would come to dance class still bleeding and my coach would provide me with band aids and lotion, though the latter only served to smear the blood further. I was able to keep my self-harm contained in more discreet areas, only placing a few grazes in more visible places when I could come up with a solid excuse as to why they were there.

31

I struggled in school as well; I had never learned well when I was expected to follow a curriculum that was primarily online. I was involved in a rigorous program that was half high school, half college. By the time I graduated high school, I was expected to also graduate with an associate's degree in computer science from the local college. Due to that, I was in courses several years ahead of my own grade level. When learning had taken place in person, that historically hadn't been a problem for me. However, this replicated my third grade experience a little too closely and I often cried over my work or neglected to get it done all together.

Belle was enrolled in the same program as me and I often spent school days at her house, hoping her work ethic would inspire me to stay on track. This plan had little to no effect on the amount of work I completed, although it did threaten Belle's laser focus on multiple occasions. I couldn't sit still for more than thirty minutes at a time and often turned my computer camera off to walk laps around Belle's dinner table. I tried often to talk to my best friend instead of working and she rightfully became exasperated with me. Even still, Belle and I were inseparable, and our friendship remained unbreakable. The pureness of a young friendship is the infinity it seems to hold.

I was at Belle's house so frequently that her parents referred to me as their third child. We often had sleepovers and played family games together. The sleepovers ended after my parents informed her parents of my lesbian identity and I was deemed a threat. Belle was questioning her own identity at the time, but I was no longer attracted to her even in an intrusive manner since I had a girlfriend. I believe I was only attracted to her in the first place because at the time, she was the only person who was aware of that vulnerable part of me. Now that I had found a community and was out publicly, it was no longer intimate knowledge.

Bronwyn was now attending the same school as me, though she was a grade ahead of me, and she was my true crush. I looked forward to seeing her face in the little square box of online lectures. I began talking to her again through texts, but of course didn't flirt with her or tell her I had feelings for her since I was committed to dating

Lydia. Bronwyn was just effortlessly beautiful; she didn't wear makeup or spend hours doing her hair she was simply naturally stunning. She had a soft calming voice and a laugh that flowed into my ears like liquid gold. She was private and that made her illusive and mysterious, like a puzzle begging to be solved. I tried repeatedly to convince myself that my feelings for her were no deeper than my feelings for Lydia, but I couldn't fall for my own lies.

As the competition season of dance approached, the threats of residential treatment commenced once more. I had lost an obvious amount of weight and was very thin, although I still found girls thinner than me to envy. My period had stopped and my puberty along with it, but now that was no longer enough. I continued to thirst for more, wanting to fade away into nothingness. I was rewarded at dance for overexerting myself and punished when my body would finally give out. My dance teacher encouraged us to dance until we dropped, telling us we weren't working hard enough if we weren't throwing up. Of course, there was typically nothing in my stomach to throw up, but I would find myself breathless and shaking after the long practices.

My dad talked to my dance teacher, asking her to encourage me to eat. She called me aside in class one day and muttered, "Your father asked me to talk to you. I guess you could stand to gain a few pounds," she paused after the unwilling statement for a moment before adding, "But keep the ballet body. A thin frame is perfect for ballet so don't lose it, just make your dad happy before he takes you out of classes."

Her sentiment didn't motivate me at all, and I continued to intentionally deprive myself of food. I attempted to lose weight in every way possible, intense workouts, ice baths to boost my metabolism, laxatives to prevent me from fully digesting the small amount of food that I did consume. On occasions, I would put so much laxative powder into a drink that it would become thick and nearly impossible to gulp down. When I inevitably got hungry, I would either chew food and spit it out or eat small amounts of condiments and seasoning, such as a spoonful of jam or a pinch of salt. My goal was to have an entirely flat chest. I didn't know whether that goal was

33

attainable so late in puberty, but I was more than willing to push myself until I found out.

After winter break, we were allowed to attend school in person with masks two days a week. People with last names starting with the letters A-K went to school on Mondays and Wednesdays while people with last names beginning with the letters L-Z attended school in person on Tuesdays and Thursdays. On days when your last name did not enable you to attend school, you continued learning online. Bronwyn and I had to attend school on different days which disappointed me, but there was nothing that could be done about it. On the other hand, Belle and I were scheduled to go to school on the same days, which meant I could continue to do virtual learning with her on the days we weren't in school.

I was glad to be able to have a break from being in my own home. My parents and I still fought often about my identity. Their religious views drove them to insist that I wasn't a lesbian and that being gay was morally wrong. I began to fear religion, staying deep in the closet at my church. I mentioned that I had a girlfriend once on accident during a small group meeting where the other girls were discussing their boyfriends, and the leader of the group called my mother to complain about my "inappropriate behavior." I was still on the worship team, but I had watched people get kicked off the team for being gay, so I was extremely careful and reserved during rehearsals and performances.

In my next lesson with Michael, I asked him, "Does God hate gay people?"

He of course, knew my sexuality and replied, "No, not at all. You should come to my church, we would never say that. I don't know why Christians believe that, but it isn't true. Are your parents still not accepting of you?"

"No," I responded. "They told me that gay people aren't God's best work."

"You should run away," he suggested. "But don't just run away without knowing where you're going, you'll get sex trafficked. You should run away to my house, and I'll keep you safe."

To my fourteen-year-old angsty self, this sounded like a perfectly reasonable idea, and I agreed to start memorizing the directions to his home. Michael had always been there for me, and he had become a father figure of sorts. He had given me advice on how to separate myself from and disown my parents to avoid getting hurt time and time again. He was a father himself with two young children, a toddler boy and an elementary school aged girl. He led the worship team at his own church and had earned himself a shining reputation in our community. My voice lessons took place at his little yellow house by the window looking out into their yard.

After we spent nearly the entire lesson talking, we sang a duet to finish the voice lesson. This particular duet had become something we sang every lesson, and it was extraordinarily inappropriate and sexual. At first, I had mumbled through the raunchy lines uncomfortably, but Michael had assured me that I was old enough to say these things now and I eventually felt comfortable singing the song at full volume with him. The lyrics asked him to slap me, pull my hair, get his ass in gear, and labeled me as "hot and pissed and on the pill" among other things. There was even a section in the middle that implied the characters were having sex mid-song. I came to love singing it with him, it made me feel so mature and grown-up. I had been fourteen when we had started singing the duet together, now I had just turned fifteen and knew every word by heart.

When we finished singing, he gave me an overly long hug, rubbing my back and promising that he would never hurt me like my parents had, before watching me walk out to my mother's car. I trusted Michael, if he said I had to run away, he was likely right. I had never seriously considered it before then, I figured I wouldn't have anywhere to go and would get caught fairly quickly. I couldn't even drive yet, so I would have to travel on foot under the coverage of the dark night and find places to hide during the day. Luckily, that problem had now been solved. I didn't exactly understand what I expected to happen, maybe I would just hide away with Michael for years and re-enter the world when I was old enough to be independent. I hadn't thought about living a life equivalent to that of a captive and being forced to hide for years, I didn't yet have the ability to fully think through such a big decision. All I knew was that an opportunity had presented itself and I would take it.

Throughout each long school day, I learned how to hide my raging hunger. When my stomach would begin to loudly rumble from emptiness, I would flex my abs to hold it back. During lunch, I did my best to keep my eyes from glaring at the people's food greedily. My own food always ended up in the trash, but I would sit in front of it for a while just to feel a sense of belonging at the table. Music was imperative to get through each day, it kept me calm and gave me something to focus on besides hunger or pain from open wounds. If I was having a particularly awful day, I would self-harm in the bathroom secretly. I never got caught despite often having splotches of blood adorning my pants.

By April, I was ready to run away and abandon my mundane and depressing life. I had memorized the directions to Michael's house and was prepared to leave my house in the middle of the night to walk there, knowing he would accept me with open arms when I arrived at his doorstep. I quietly waited for the perfect opportunity to arrive. I had to be mad enough to walk out, there had to be a fight leading up to my disappearance to ensure I wouldn't feel bad or regret it.

Before my next lesson, when I planned to inform Michael that I was ready to run away, my parents and I received an email from Michael's wife stating:

Hi everyone, it's Danielle.

I am writing this email with a heavy heart. These last two weeks have been very traumatic for our family. While I won't go into details about the events surrounding our trauma, we are counting our blessings that Mike is here with us, and our family will get through the upcoming dark times with a renewed sense of strength and support for the man Mike truly is.

We decided that it is in the best interest of our family to close Schneider Music Studio indefinitely. We will return April payments we already received and will not accept any future payments. After this email is sent, we will close down this email address. Mike no longer has access to his phone and will no longer have the number associated with it. We ask that you please respect our family, as you always have, and not reach out for further information.

We hope that you remember Mike for the legacy he truly built, not what may be said. He is a passionate educator, doting father, loving husband and faithful follower of Christ. He is also human and has his limits and faults. He worked ceaselessly to share his love of music with all he met, and it is my personal hope that you will continue to build and strengthen that love of music within your student.

In love and peace,

Danielle

My father was convinced Michael had attempted suicide and I held the same belief. I was distraught, not only had I lost my opportunity to run away, but an adult I trusted and cared about had attempted suicide. I was almost jealous in a way of the bravery it must have taken to attempt; I had been suicidal for a while but hadn't yet attempted to take my life. I had been saving up pills in a small bag hidden in my desk in hopes that I would eventually take them all at once and die. I decided to follow Michael and take the pills I had saved up late that night.

I went to school, feeling everything and nothing simultaneously. I warned Lydia that I was going to take the pills that night and she of course attempted to persuade me not to. It was too late, I had already made my decision. If this world wasn't good enough for Michael to live in, it certainly wasn't fit for me to live in either. That night, I took the cocktail of aspirin, Zoloft, ibuprofen, and Tylenol I had collected, taking each pill one by one as I had a hard time swallowing them. I went to sleep immediately, praying that I would never again wake up.

I did wake up the following morning, feeling incredibly ill. I called down the hallway from my bed, "Mom, I'm sick today! I'm staying home from school!"

My mother arrived at my door and looked me over, "You look ghostly pale!" she exclaimed.

I managed to run to the bathroom and get to the toilet before I began dry heaving. My head was spinning, and I wasn't sure how long I would be able to stay conscious. My dad knocked at the door, yelling at me to hurry up. I exited the bathroom, hardly able to walk due to the shaking that had overcome my entire body and found my way to the downstairs couch. I told my parents that my blood sugar must have been low and asked for some sugar packets to eat. I consumed them and spent the remainder of the day at home slowly recovering. I never told my parents the truth about what had happened, only my close friends knew.

By the summer of that year, I had come to terms with the fact that I wasn't a girl but I still wasn't willing to say I was a boy. I began asking for a "Leonardo DiCaprio" haircut and to wear masculine clothes. My parents refused both, insisting that I was a girl and would wear girl's clothes. I began stealing my brother's old clothes since the clothes he had outgrown were around my size. He began helping me, going through his clothes and putting the ones I was allowed to have in bags with drawings of pride flags on them. It was sweet, it reminded me that we would always be there for each other. I was still forced to wear feminine clothes around extended family or for special events, but on a regular basis I refused to wear anything besides the hand me downs I received from my brother.

I knew dance wouldn't be an ideal environment for me to be able to express my newfound gender identity as it was a very strictly gendered environment. I started wishing I had never joined dance at all and hated the tights and leotards I had to wear more and more. I enjoyed dancing more than anything, it simply wasn't an environment where I could be myself. One day, my opportunity to quit appeared in front of me quite suddenly. We were doing a group improvisation piece during practice, and as I stood with my leg extended high in the air, the knee I stood on came out from under me.

I fell onto the ground and was unable to move my leg from its bent position. I looked at it for a moment and realized that my knee was out of its socket, sitting instead on the outside of my leg. I laid down and tried not to cry as the other girls were filed out of the room with a mixture of shock and disgust on their faces. An ambulance was called, and the EMT's placed an IV in me with Fentanyl flowing throw it to decrease the pain I was in. I was in such intense pain that I wasn't even sure what to do, I hit my head and rocked it side to side rhythmically. I called Lydia in the ambulance to explain what happened before I arrived at the hospital with my dad. After three hours, my knee was put back in place and I was sent home with crutches and a brace to keep my knee straight.

Chapter Five: Lead Flies

"Did you get enough love, my little dove? Why do you cry?"

-Sufjan Stevens

A few days after I dislocated my knee, my request to get my hair cut was finally granted. My mom took me to her friend's salon and together they talked me into getting a bob rather than a boy's haircut. I knew I wouldn't be allowed to get my hair cut as short as I wanted to, but I found myself disappointed. I was still happier with my hair just brushing my shoulders than I had been with it grazing my waist. I was attending church at that time and contemplating returning to dance after I recovered, so a bob was the safer option at the time anyways.

I had since been informed by another student of Michael's what had really happened. He was in jail for grooming kids. Soon, news articles began coming out and I was shocked to learn more and more about what had actually occurred. He had been indicted with 135 counts of child pornography possession, six counts of sexual assault with a minor between the ages of thirteen and seventeen, and one count of enticing a child to remove their clothing. I was shocked, Michael had been my safe space. I had trusted him entirely, whatever he said to me had been treated as the truth. I wasn't able to fully process it, but I had the itching sensation that I hadn't been safe from him either.

A couple of days before school was scheduled to begin, it was time to take my sophomore photos for the yearbook. I asked to wear masculine clothes, but my mom responded, "Grandma doesn't want a picture of you looking like a boy on her fridge," and I was placed in a tight striped top with a butterfly on it and skinny jeans. An overwhelming wave of dysphoria threatened to crush me, but I attempted to keep my composure. I crutched into the school on the verge of tears and put on a smile as the camera flashed, capturing everything I hated about myself and solidifying it as my identity in a book for years to come. I tried not to think about my friends looking in the yearbook with their future children and pointing to that picture to show them who I was. It wasn't who I was.

School was fully in person for the first time in over a year, though we all had to wear masks. I enjoyed wearing masks knowing that it shielded half of me from the glaring eyes of the world. I was almost saddened that the rest of me couldn't be hidden so easily. I was short, only five feet tall, but five feet isn't invisible. I certainly tried my best to be unseen and unheard, but simply being a body in a room is harder than one might think.

On the first day of school, my first hour teacher called my name out for attendance, "Felicity Laurence?"

"Here! I actually go by..." I hesitated. I had been trying out the name Devyn for a few weeks, but it didn't seem to fit me. I thought of the list of names I had come up with for myself: Briar, Fallon, Killian, and, "Faber. I go by Faber," I decided.

I continued introducing myself as Faber in each of my classes, informing my friends of the sudden name decision. Faber was derived from the name of my favorite drawing pencils, Faber Castell. I was an avid artist with a specialty in realism and relied on Faber Castell pencils as they had been around for centuries. They had even been mentioned in my favorite book, written in the Civil War era, entitled "Little Women." I had always seen myself in the gentle character Beth and the misfit sister Jo who didn't seem to belong with the other girls. I had loved the book since second grade and watched the movie religiously.

I got into the rhythm of things quickly. I crutched out of history class everyday beside a popular girl named Daisy, I was flattered that she paid attention to me. I sat next to Bronwyn in Pre-Calculus, and it kept me on my best behavior, I was always trying to do well to impress her. Every day, she would take my crutches from me after I sat down and lay them against the nearest counter. She was selfless in that way, always doing what she could to help people. Choir was my favorite class, I enjoyed the melodies as they flowed through my body, each harmony embracing me with its warmth. I was in the top choir with Bronwyn, typically reserved for juniors and seniors.

Lydia and I broke up early in the year. I had stopped bending to her every need and ruining my sleep schedule to take care of her. She felt neglected and broke up with me and I experienced a wave of relief. She asked me to get back together with her shortly afterwards, but I refused. Not only did I not want her as a liability anymore, but I also was in the process of figuring out my gender identity and dating a lesbian made me feel obligated to keep at least some resemblance of a girl. I knew being tied down was only preventing me from figuring myself out and I needed to be free of both responsibility and obligation.

October 8th was homecoming and I planned to go with Belle. I informed my parents that I would not be wearing a dress under any circumstances, and they were livid. They shot back that if I didn't wear a dress, I couldn't go. I refused. I was not going to embarrass myself by wearing a dress. I was not going to go through one more special occasion in *my* life painting a picture of what my parents wished I was. I fought with them a few times before deciding that I wouldn't go. I made a secondary plan, a plan to kill myself on the night of homecoming. I couldn't be who I was, and I was tired. I was exhausted by the limitations placed on me. If I couldn't be who I wanted to be for one night, I would ensure it was the final night of my life.

I became even more withdrawn at school, pretending to be occupied by my phone instead of conversing with people. Daisy stopped paying attention to me and I would follow close beside her, silently begging her to talk to me just one more time. I spent every night talking Lydia down from suicide even though we had broken up. I had tried contacting her mom, but she had simply said it was wonderful that Lydia had found an outlet through me. I also now had the responsibility of talking her friend Kage down from suicide on a nightly basis. She had introduced him to me a while back when she needed help convincing him to stay on the Earth and he had relied on me ever since. He spent hours detailing his past suicide attempts to me and threatening to attempt again.

On the night of September 30th, I stayed up until 2 a.m. begging Kage not to kill himself. He explained to me how his body was distorted from his past attempts and his self-mutilation and instructed me to go to bed. When I asked him to promise me he would still be alive in the morning, he simply responded, "Lead flies when need be, but tired minds need rest." I texted him for another half hour before finally surrendering to my tiredness and allowing myself to go to sleep.

The next morning, I texted to check on him. I monitored my phone throughout the school day as each hour passed without a response. I started to panic, it was so selfish of me to go to sleep when I was supposed to save him. If he had killed himself, I never would have been able to forgive myself. I shouldn't have gone to sleep. I should have stayed up all night if that's what it took. I had tried to convince him to call a hotline, I had tried to get his address so I could call the police. What more could I have done? In the moment, it seemed as though I could have done infinitely more than I had.

By the time I got to Pre-Calculus, tears were forming in my eyes and I could feel myself slowly losing my ability to hold myself together. I waited until Bronwyn had finished taking her notes, not wanting to affect her grade in any way, before asking, "Can we go somewhere?"

She nodded, got up, and handed me my crutches. We left the class and started walking down the hall. "Why don't we go downstairs and sit on the bench for a little while?" she suggested.

I agreed and we took the elevator downstairs before sitting on the bench by the stairs. I began crying immediately, "I think he's dead, Bronwyn. I think he's dead and it's all my fault! I should never have gone to sleep. I was just so tired. I've been staying awake until the morning for weeks now trying to talk him out of it. I don't know why he chose me to save him, I can't even save myself. I don't understand!"

Bronwyn shifted and looked into my eyes before calmly stating, "It seems like you've been holding onto this for a while now." She always knew what to say, she was so perfect. She didn't even know who I was talking about and she still knew what to say. She was so perfect and I was such a mess.

43

My hands began to seize up into unmovable fists as I sobbed, and it became hard to breathe. "I don't want to die, I just want to disappear. I wish I had never been born, then I wouldn't have to hurt anyone by not existing. Now I'm here and my choice to die would hurt so many people. My mom says I'm never happy, I got my hair cut and I'm still not happy, I wear boy's clothes and I'm still not happy, maybe she's right. I don't have any real friends, I try not to talk to people."

"If it makes you feel any better, I'm glad we get to be friends," she soothed.

"I want to believe you, but I just can't," I choked. I couldn't move my hands anymore, the unvoluntary fists were so tight that it physically hurt. I was starting to lose myself, becoming dizzy from the lack of air and the exertion of crying so hard. My phone buzzed and I peered at the text. "It's my mom, can you text her back for me please? I don't want her to know what's going on, it will only make it worse."

She picked up my phone, "What do you want me to say?"

"Tell her I'm studying for a math test," I instructed.

"And she can't know about this because it will make it worse?" she confirmed uncomfortably.

"No, she can't know" I replied. "She'll come pick me up and I need you right now, not her. I don't want to go home. I have to be a girl at home and we always fight about it. Please don't make me go home!"

Bronwyn texted my mother silently and watched me as I slowly became more and more distraught. Each time I began to pull myself together, I fell apart once more into even more pieces.

"My hands hurt!" I sobbed in between fits of gasping for air.

"Which one hurts more?" she asked gently.

"My left," I clarified. She sat on the left of me and took my hand in hers, gently rubbing it in an attempt to relieve some of the tension. "This is going to end, right? This has to end eventually?"

44

"I promise it will end," she assured me.

We sat on that bench for over two hours as she took turns rubbing each of my fists. I would shake my head every now and then to clear it of a thought only to share what I had been thinking with her. Eventually, I was able to stop crying and told her I needed to use the restroom. I couldn't walk without my crutches, and I was on the verge of passing out, so she walked me there with my arm around her shoulders. I couldn't unbutton my pants with my hands being incapacitated, so she had to do it for me. Luckily, I was able to do everything else in the privacy of a stall.

Bronwyn walked me out to her red minivan in the same fashion she had walked me to the bathroom, helped me into the passenger's seat, and buckled me in before driving me to her house. I felt a pungent love for her, this beautiful, perfect, selfless girl. I didn't even understand how she was human, she had to be secretly among the gods. She was certainly a god to me in that moment, an omnipotent being always watching over flawed mortals like me. Even if I were to live a thousand lifetimes, I would still never possess the amount of goodness she held in her pinkie finger.

I had never been to Bronwyn's home, and I limped inside nervously. Her mom stood at the counter upstairs washing dishes and greeted me by saying, "Hello, Faber!"

A parent had never used my name before, it was entirely unprecedented. I didn't even have to inform her of my name, she just knew it. I processed it for a moment before responding, "Hello, Mrs. Gorecki."

Bronwyn's large dog came running up to me and I began to stroke her head with a hand that was still stuck in a balled-up position. We went to Bronwyn's room, which was the same shade of lilac as my own, and sat on her bed. "Since you don't want to go home, would you like to stay the night?" she offered.

"That would be amazing!" I replied. "Is your house always this peaceful?"

She hesitated for a moment before replying, "Yes."

I texted my parents using my fists asking if I could spend the night at Bronwyn's house. A few minutes later, my phone started ringing and I answered. I was surprised to hear my grandma's voice on the other end of the line, I had forgotten she was visiting. "Felicity?"

I responded to my old name tiredly, "Grandma, can I stay the night at Bronwyn's house please?"

"Absolutely not!" she answered sternly. "You have taken this way too far, young lady. You said you were studying and now you've missed our family dinner, worried your parents, and lied about where you were!"

The phone was on speaker since I couldn't hold it in my fists, and I looked at Bronwyn with tears in my eyes. She responded to the rest of the call, telling my father her address so he could pick me up and hanging the phone up for me. "Will you come outside with me so he won't yell at me when I ask to stay?" I asked her.

"Sure," she agreed.

Ten minutes later, we watched his car pull in and I crutched out of her house. Her mom bid me goodbye as Bronwyn walked outside with me. I had planned to protest my father picking me up and ask to stay, but at the last second, I decided to quietly leave. I couldn't bear to bring chaos to this serene place, I couldn't infect this perfection with my messiness.

After that day, I blocked both Lydia and Kage without a warning. I was too tired to support them anymore. As someone who had been on both ends of the situation, I understood people who needed a bit of support every once and a while, but once it became a daily occurrence and they refused to seek any other resources, it had gone too far. Everyone deserves a solid support system, but that system cannot be one teenage kid hundreds of miles away. I often utilized helplines and crisis lines when I needed to talk about something I felt was too heavy for my friends. On occasion, I still made mistakes and put something on my friends that they shouldn't have had to worry about, like my breakdown in front of Bronwyn, but I was working diligently to decrease those incidents.

I admitted to Bronwyn that I had a crush on her late one evening. She commended me for the bravery it took to tell her and replied that she only saw me as a friend, and she hoped our friendship didn't change. It did change for a few weeks as I avoided her out of shame, but soon I realized I loved having Bronwyn as a friend more than anything and dating would likely ruin that bond. Before long, we were talking to each other again and became closer than ever. It took a while for my romantic feelings towards her to fade, but slowly and surely, they disappeared entirely.

Bronwyn recruited me into the mock trial team at school. In the beginning, I had only joined to spend more time with her, but as soon as it began, I found myself enjoying the challenges it brought. It was stimulating and entertaining. We were split into six teams, three defense teams and three prosecution teams. Each team was given the same packet full of sworn statements from fake witnesses portraying both sides of the claim, along with evidence. From there, each team had to develop a theme and theory for the case, choose two witnesses to portray, and write out an entire trial. I was assigned to be a witness rather than an attorney and found quick success with my writing skills on direct examinations and quick thinking during cross examinations. I was frequently complimented by the coaches and was viewed as a rising star of sorts.

The hardest time of the year for me was the winter. Something about it was so desolate and lonely. I refused to listen to Christmas music, it infuriated me. I couldn't feel the joy of the holidays and I was jealous of those who could. My birthday is on December 7, and I dreaded it immensely. Sixteen years old seemed too mature for me, I wasn't ready to grow up. I longed to be a child again and couldn't process that I was slowly becoming a functioning adult in society. I often looked in the mirror, hoping to see baby teeth and chubby toddler cheeks again, only to find dark circles under my eyes and a well-defined jawline.

I was utterly miserable, crying through my entire birthday and self-harming on Christmas Eve rather than anticipating presents. I had truly become the child who never smiled. I no longer laughed or sang or danced, I simply wallowed in my desolation. I no longer cared what I received for Christmas and had made a list full of items I neither wanted nor needed. They were things I remembered finding joy in, sketchbooks, art supplies, technology, but I felt disappointingly neutral about it all at that point. The holidays came and went, and I figured out I was a boy right before the New Year began.

After the holidays, mock trial began to become a true commitment. We had competitions nearly every weekend. I received a few awards for my skills as a witness, but our team as a whole often got beaten by schools with more resources to pour into their teams. Even though we were underdogs, we practiced efficiently and frequently to sharpen our skills. My attorney and I often stayed up late into the night on phone calls revising our direct examination to minimize possible objections and pull at heartstrings. Once we had perfected it, we were objected to for our probative narrative and had to start from scratch. We were beaten down for a moment but sprang back up with excitement and drafted a new direct examination quickly. I was one of the top ten team members and was the only sophomore to be on the worshipped state competition team.

Tensions at my house were rising steadily. My parents suspected me of self-harming and would do anything to find out. They often tried to catch me off guard and lift up my sleeves, but my reflexes were always quicker, and I wouldn't let them see. One day, my dad walked into my room when we were alone and demanded for me show him my arms. I started discreetly filming him on my phone as he became louder and more aggressive, out of fear. He seemed a bit drunk, a few of his sentences were more of a jumble of syllables and words than actual sentences.   He held my ankles down to the bed as I squirmed around trying to escape. It was futile, he was angry and strong. He continued to yell at me, reaching for my sleeves, demanding to see my arms, and squeezing my ankles tighter each time I squirmed. I held back tears as I begged him to go away and gave up trying to escape from his grasp. He began lunging at me and I cried in fear as he claimed he wasn't doing anything. By the time my mother came into the room to save me, he had both of my legs held to his chest with one arm and was just about to reach my sleeve with the other. I was terrified, I hated knowing that he was stronger than me. He claimed no wrongdoing, and I was grateful when my mother removed him from the room. I had caught the entire interaction on video, and it was reported to CPS but nothing came of it.

Just as the mock trial season ended, musical season began. I auditioned for my first male role, a young boy by the name of Jojo, and surprisingly got the role! I gained a sudden popularity in the niche group of theater kids and went from a quiet unknown sophomore to someone everyone wanted to be friends with overnight. I shared with my newfound friends the amount of dysphoria my hair was causing me. I often sat in front of the mirror at night with my hair sectioned perfectly and clippers in my hands praying for the courage to turn them on and cut my hair myself. I had been begging my parents to let me cut my hair like a boy, but they were insistent in their refusal. One of my new friends, Kinsley, offered to drive me to a barber in her van. I was elated by the idea and went to ask permission from the directors of the musical.

I didn't expect it to be a source of conflict as I was playing a male role and had informed my directors about my struggles with gender dysphoria in the past. I was surprised to be met with pushback to my request. The directors claimed my bob haircut made me appear innocent and it was part of their vision for me to remain the way I was. I questioned why they would want a boy character to look like a girl but wasn't skilled at standing up to authority figures and kept my confusion quiet. I informed my friends of their response, and soon rumors began to spread that the directors were transphobic.

During choir class, the teacher and music director, Ms. Peters, called me into her office, leaving the class to watch a movie on the smartboard. When I walked into her office, I was greeted by the other director, the infamous Ms. Kingston. I was offered a seat by the door across from both of them and sat in it, closing the door behind me.

"Faber, we need to talk," Ms. Peters began gently.

"There are rumors going around that we're transphobic," Ms. Kingston interjected bluntly. "If you know anything about us, you know that isn't true. I have more gay friends than straight friends!"

"We're just offended to hear that you haven't been defending us at all, it isn't fair to us. This really is a relationship ruiner, we don't like gossip," Ms. Peters added.

Tears began to well up in my eyes, "I-"

"I don't even think you know where these rumors are coming from, so I don't think it's your fault, but you need to stand up for us!" Ms. Kingston objected.

"If we had known the haircut was related to your dysphoria, of course we would have said yes. You never told us." But I had, hadn't I?

When the meeting concluded, I was in tears over being cornered and ran out of the class to recover in the restroom. I splashed water in my face and managed to get the tears to stop flowing before I turned to see that Kinsley had followed me in.

"Are you ok, buddy?" she asked.

I was nervous one of the directors had followed behind me as well, so I decided to choose my words carefully. "Yeah, nothing bad happened. I just got a little overwhelmed. I just need to pull myself together."

"I get that," she chirped. "Do you want me to go back to class or stay with you?"

"You can stay, I'll only be a few more minutes," I assured her shakily.

Though the confrontational feeling of the meeting had brought me to tears, what came of it was that I was allowed to cut my hair. I gave my parents one final chance to take me themselves and gave them a fair warning that I was going to move forward with or without them.

Once it was clear that they would not be taking me, Kinsley, Bronwyn, and I formed a plan. I was extremely grateful that the two of them were willing to help me. Both of them were able to drive, Kinsley was a senior and Bronwyn a junior at the time.

After school the following day, Kinsley drove me in her van, Sandy, to Target. She had to leave for work after walking around with me for a little while. I bought supplies I expected to need for my new haircut, combs to replace my brush and a few different styling products. When I finished shopping, I walked the short distance to the nearest hair salon, crossing roads and adjusting my heavy backpack on my shoulders. I got in, set my bag down, and was seated in a chair quickly.

I explained that I wanted a boy haircut and showed a few reference pictures, explaining which qualities I liked and didn't like in each one. I knew my hair couldn't be too short because it was thin and blonde, making it hard to see if there wasn't enough of it. The stylist suggested a size 8 clipper guard for the back and sides and bangs that just reached the top of my eyebrows, it sounded perfect to me. After shaving the bottom half of my head with the clippers, he paused to confirm that I was ready to go through with this. I had been waiting for years, and I eagerly encouraged him to finish the job. I couldn't stop smiling, I felt so free and happy.

When he was finished, he put a sticky substance in my hair that made it look funny and I was almost worried I didn't like it. I pulled out the cash I had saved up from my backpack and paid him. I bought another hair styling product and talked to the man at the checkout, who also happened to be transgender, for a while. Soon, Bronwyn's red minivan had pulled into the parking lot, and I skipped out of the store to claim my place in the passenger's seat.

"I know it looks a little funny right now," I began. "He put some weird sticky stuff in my hair, it looked great before. Don't worry, it will look way better at school tomorrow."

"It's so short!" Bronwyn squealed.

"I know! I feel so much better now!" I exclaimed. Bronwyn drove me home in the dark of the evening, playing music quietly as we talked.

When I walked in the house, I was relieved to not see any of my family members on my way to the bathroom. I quickly touched up my hair to my liking with scissors, rounding it a bit more and squaring the sideburns. I took a hot shower to rinse the product out of my hair. I took much longer than I typically did, massaging my head repeatedly just to feel the short length of my hair and verify that it was real. When I got out of the shower and looked in the mirror, I was astounded by my own reflection. I really looked like a boy! I finally saw the boy I had waited so many years to see in the mirror. I got dressed and took pictures to capture the moment before staring at myself more and playing around with my hair. It was everything I had ever wanted and more.

Chapter Six: Dark Age

"And I've been meaning to tell you, I think your house is haunted. Your dad is always mad, and that must be why. And I think you should come live with me, and we can be pirates. Then you won't have to cry or hide in the closet."

- Taylor Swift

Not long before my sophomore year ended, my business law class took a trip to the local courthouse to observe trials. Since all trials besides juvenile court were public trials, we were free to enter and exit courtrooms as we pleased. I bounced between a few trials, not finding any of them particularly interesting. As I scanned the lists of trials outside of each door, I spotted the name "Michael D. Schneider." I didn't believe it was possible that the Michael I knew had court on the same day I was in the courthouse, so I decided to see for myself if it was him.

I entered the courtroom in my suit and tie and sat on one of the benches on the left side of the room. The person in front of me looked like his wife Danielle, but it was hard to tell from behind. I truly didn't believe my luck, or misfortune, to have a scheduled trip to the courthouse on Michael's court date. The judge summoned him, and he entered the room from a hallway on the side of the room. His hands were shackled to his waist, and he had shaved both his head and his beard. I immediately began shaking intensely and I could feel my heart clanging against my ribcage as if it were a mallet pounding on a gong. I clutched my heart, and my vision went black just as he turned to look at his wife sitting in front of me.

The next thing I knew, I was running down the long staircase to find my business law teacher. My vision returned as I ran, allowing me to look down at my shaking hands. I found my teacher and stayed by his side for the remainder of the visit, no longer interested in exploring on my own. The last time I had seen Michael was in his mugshot that lived in the photo album of my phone. It had been a year since I had seen him in person, it had felt as though he had left the

Earth entirely. But he hadn't, and at that moment, he was closer to me than he had been in a long time.

I participated in summer theatre with Bronwyn as I did every year. The musical was Grease, and Bronwyn and I were both in the ensemble so we were able to spend the majority of our time together. During one performance, I had forgotten to bandage my leg where I had recently self-harmed. I looked down while I was on stage and saw a large patch of blood soaking through my pants, so large it looked as though I had been shot in the leg. I quickly shielded my leg from the view of the audience and turned to the person nearest to me, a gentle and pretty girl named Layla, and asked her to exit the stage with me so it would look planned. She agreed, and we walked off stage together.

Once we were backstage, I pointed to my leg to explain the urgency in my request to leave and Layla gasped. She led me to the bathroom and told me, "I'll go get the backstage mom for you, stay here!"

I looked at my slicked back 50's hairstyle in the mirror and waited nervously for Layla to return. The backstage mom, Jody, was very kind and had helped me through a panic attack the previous year. She came into the bathroom, bearing new pants and held gauze to my leg until the bleeding was controlled enough to bandage it. She told me about how she used to help her own daughter through self-harm and I felt a small pang in my heart. She promised not to tell anyone about what had happened and took my pants to her own home to wash to ensure my parents wouldn't find out. I was extremely grateful and never told anyone else about the encounter.

School began in a week, and Belle and I had the perfect junior year planned out. We were going to carpool to school every day, go to the gym, and study together. Now that we had our drivers' licenses, we were going to do everything together. We had planned this all after realizing that we would miss riding the bus together like we did sophomore year. We had sat together, waited in uncomfortable weather for the bus to show up, and listened to music together during the ride every single day.

August 15, 2022, I rolled out of my bed to see more notifications on my phone than usual. They were texts sent from Belle's sister's phone:

Hi this is Belle please respond asap

My parents know you are trans and have basically forbade me from seeing you

I'm so sorry

They think something made me how I am and it was something's fault and yelled at me

Again please respond asap

Forbade? I had been friends with Belle since seventh grade. Not just friends, best friends. I was over at her house so often her parents joked that I was their third child. We hadn't been able to have sleepovers since my parents told her parents that I liked girls, but besides that I thought I had a good relationship with her entire family. I began to cry and shake, everything we had planned, everything that used to be, it was all over. I typed out a shaky reply:

I don't know how to respond to that other than I'm sorry

No new texts appeared and I defeatedly got ready to go to work. I had just gotten a job at a restaurant and over the past few weeks I had become familiarized with my tasks. I enjoyed knowing that I was earning money more than the job itself. I wasn't a particularly greedy person, but I was very money motivated nonetheless. I worked my shifts quietly, making sandwiches as quickly and efficiently as I was able to and doing my best to please my managers.

Before long, school began and I got into a routine. I based the entirety of my day around seeing Bronwyn, feeling she was the only friend I had left. Her mother had been the first parent to use my real name, her parents wouldn't hurt me the way Belle's had. I still saw Belle at school, I tried to pretend everything was fine, but I felt entirely distanced from her. We were still in the STEM cohort together, I had a

55

lot of classes with her. We didn't laugh like we used to, my laughter was shallow and apathetic around her. I couldn't feel anything but a tender ache when we were together. A fresh wound to the heart stings more than one to the flesh.

I became close with a few of my coworkers, desperate to fill the void Belle had left. I first bonded with Callie, a tall brunette girl, who had a soothing sweet voice and was strikingly beautiful. I also became close with her friend Devyn, a tall, freckled girl adorned with crystals and a pleasing musty aroma. Finally, Devyn introduced me to her friend from school, Jolene, who was hired soon after me. Jolene had an irresistible pull to her, but you wouldn't want to be on her bad side. Seeing these coworkers provided me with something to look forward to during the painfully long shifts I worked.

From the beginning of the year, I fell into a routine of working thirty hours a week. I typically worked six days a week, occasionally all seven. It took a toll on me, I fell asleep in class often, especially in the beginning of the year. I was in a constant cycle of exhaustion; I had no place to rest. My home was a war zone, it was better to fight through shifts and school days than to fight with my parents. I often felt as though I had no home at all, my days were built to avoid the place entirely.

I stopped eating during my long shifts and at school, having only a small snack at the end of each day. A few crackers was all I needed to settle my rumbling stomach. I grew used to the hunger pains, so used to them I hardly felt them at all. I no longer had to flex my stomach muscles to prevent the rumbling from escaping, it no longer even came until the very end of each day when I was alone. I truly believed that the less I ate, the more masculine I would feel. I starved myself more than I ever had in the past. I saw no difference when I looked in the mirror, but I believed it would work eventually and kept my eating minimal.

Early in the school year, my father and I got into an argument about my transition. I told him how I planned on starting testosterone when I turned eighteen as he didn't believe I could do it, and he was upset when he realized I could.

"If you start testosterone under this roof, you'll have to ask your mother whether you can still live here! At that point, you are going way beyond the rules of this house!" he threatened.

My father was a loose cannon, a somewhat unpredictable person. I never knew whether his angry threats were made in honesty or to shut me up, so I chose to take each one seriously to prevent surprises. I hated surprises. I wanted to leave my house as quickly as possible, but I wanted it to be my choice. I didn't want to be kicked out when I wasn't ready to afford living expenses. On the other hand, I couldn't force myself to wait any longer to transition than I had to, it would be torturous and reckless in a way. I decided that I would begin to work even more to save up money in case of a catastrophe.

I sat on the corner of the couch as my father continued to detail what would happen if I decided to start testosterone while under his roof. "Boys don't cry," a lyric from a song I listened to, reverberated in my head as I felt the sting of tears welling up within me. I was used to feeling small around my father, but it was different now that I had the added pressure of proving my masculinity to him. I couldn't cry in front of him anymore, it would only prove in his mind that I was just a confused little girl. My brother was allowed to cry without my father bringing his masculinity into question, but it was different for me. Every second of my life was a battle of proving myself.

After that day, I stopped blowing my paychecks and started saving the majority of my money, only spending a small portion of my earnings on niceties. I worked obsessively, saving up as much money as I could in fear of winding up on the streets before I even graduated high school. I knew my dad often said things in anger that he didn't mean, but the threat was very real to me, and I couldn't ignore its looming presence. I wished I lived in a different house. I wished I had a different family.

In school, I had periods where I was able to leave campus and I began utilizing them to attend Michael's court dates which were typically held in the morning. It occurred to me that I had once been his nymph, a teenage girl playing the part of Lolita unknowingly. He likely didn't recognize me with my short hair that accentuated my baby face when I sat in his court rooms, watching silently. I never heard him speak, his attorney spoke on his behalf. Both of us sat in mirrored silence, the difference between us being that his chains were physical and mine were not. He had programmed me, changed the wiring of my mind completely without my permission and whether I knew it or not, I was eternally tied to him.

I stopped blacking out every time I went to watch the trials. My mind was able to neutralize itself enough for me to sit in the room anxiously tapping my leg. Occasionally, my visits made me late to class since no phones were allowed in the courthouse and clocks were sparce. I didn't dress up when I visited on my own, I wore my typical school clothes, a hoodie and jeans. A few times I was asked if I was there to attend my own trial, to which I tried not to giggle at the accusation as I reported that I was merely observing. Sometimes I wanted to run up to Michael and hug him, I wasn't exactly sure why. My feelings about the whole situation were difficult to decipher. They twisted and tangled and ebbed and flowed.

I found out that Callie's sister, Juliet, had been the "whistleblower" victim, the person who alerted the police to Michael's wrongdoings. I went over to Callie's house after a long day of work and sat upstairs in her room. She changed clothes and I closed my eyes to respect her privacy, she insisted that I didn't have to, but I was more comfortable that way. I always felt wrong when I saw people naked, like a terrible person. When I first came out, I had been treated as a predator of sorts, and it stuck with me. I couldn't stand to see people in vulnerable situations, even on the television.

Callie, on the other hand, was extremely comfortable with vulnerability. She ducked down under her bed after changing and pulled out a pink vibrator, "I should teach you how to masturbate!" she suggested.

Callie attended a catholic school, but she was far from catholic. I stared at her in horror, I wasn't sure how she planned to teach me, but it immediately reminded me of my old internet friend Cassie. Our friendship had quickly turned creepy before Michael had gone to jail and I had cut contact with her. She had sent me multiple links to sex toys and insisted that I learned how to masturbate with them despite my discomfort. I wasn't interested in anything sexual, so I had to stop communicating with her once it became all she wanted to talk about with me.

"No thanks," I responded awkwardly.

"Okay, do you want to talk to Juliet? She heard about you, and she wanted to talk to you about Michael." she informed me.

I had never talked to Juliet before, but I was eager to find out more of the story and put my own pieces together, so I agreed. She put Juliet on speaker phone, leaving me in her room with a bag of communion crackers to snack on while she went downstairs to hang out Devyn and Jolene. I found out that Michael had taken Juliet to buy sex toys, alcohol, and lingerie. He had gotten her drunk and assaulted her on multiple occasions. Our stories bore uncanny similarities, she had also identified as a lesbian at the time and the events that had happened to me was the beginning of it all for her. We had both been in vulnerable situations with our families, which he had preyed on and made worse.

When we connected the timelines, things became even more scary. She had cut ties with Michael shortly before I began taking lessons with him. When he asked me to run away to his house, the investigation against him had been recently opened. She theorized that he planned on taking me with him to run away from the police. Perhaps it was his plan to take advantage of one last child before he was put behind bars, a desperate final attempt. It likely wouldn't have lasted long, but unthinkable things would have occurred had he been able to kidnap me. I felt like such an imbecile for even considering his suggestion to run away to him. He had promised to keep me safe when he himself had been dangerous all along.

On one October evening, I went down to the basement to talk to my father. He sat on the couch, watching TV. As I approached, he shouted, "If it's about that transgender shit, I don't want to hear it!"

"But..." I began to protest.

"No! I'm not spending a minute of my day listening to it!" his voice raised further. "I would rather leave this earth than have a transgender child. I would rather leave this earth!"

I sat on the carpeted stairs as tears began to form in my eyes, "Dad..."

"Get away from me!" he screamed as if the Devil himself were present. "Get away from me! Get away from me! Get away from me!"

He turned towards me and moved to get up, I quickly ran up the stairs afraid that he would hurt me. I locked myself in my room and began to cry profusely. I had been suicidal for years and never, *never*, had I blamed it on anyone. It was a pain far too great for me to process. When had I gone from his child, his pride and joy, to something so wretched and evil that he'd rather die than have me as his child?

I hardly had time to let the events of the evening sink in before I heard rustling in the closet on the other side of the wall, my parents' closet where the guns were kept. I began weeping harder yet quieter to listen to my surroundings. I was sure he was going to attempt to kill himself. I didn't want to live with my dad anymore, but I didn't want him dead and certainly not after declaring that it was my fault. I brewed in my terror alone, unsure of what was to come. A few minutes passed by quietly as I waited to hear a bang or footsteps approaching my door. Then the footsteps came.

I heard my mother's voice at my door, "Felicity, open the door. What's going on?"

It had been her in the closet. I began to sob loudly, feeling safe once more, knowing she was finally home from work and I was no longer alone with him. I unlocked the door after several more prompts, revealing my reddened eyes and swollen face. I walked to stand in front of my desk and beside my bed, turning my face to the wall so she could no longer see my pain.

"He said he wanted to kill himself because of me!" I sobbed to her.

She began to rub my back, but I screamed upon her touch. I didn't want to be touched by anyone. Nobody I loved was safe and surely my mother would turn on me just as quickly as my father had or as secretly as Michael had, even I wasn't safe towards myself. I howled in pain, letting my salty tears drop into my mouth.

She hushed me and I cried back, "You don't say that to your child!"

I cried the rest of the night and at school the following day. I told Bronwyn what had happened of course and requested a hug from her before I left class to cry once more. If the tears I shed had been collected, they would have filled oceans. My life was completely and utterly miserable. My tender heart had been ripped to shreds once again and I was left to pick up the pieces. I jumped at every click and loud sound that reached my ears when I was at home, afraid my father was going to kill himself. It was a miserable existence that I tried to drown out through insane hours at work.

Thanksgiving approached quickly, a holiday I thoroughly dreaded. The entirety of it revolved around eating, a highly stressful and avoided activity for me. I had been slowly whittling away at the amount of food I ate each day. I couldn't bear people watching me eat, it was all done in secrecy. The idea of sitting at a large family gathering with mountains of food in front of me seemed almost torturous. For years, I had been the person with a nearly empty plate every year and it was almost expected of me, but still the event conjured up severe anxiety.

My family traveled to my grandparents' house in Michigan, as we had every year before, to celebrate. The entire weekend was awful with people commenting that I looked "gaunt," "ghostly," "sick," and "like a corpse." Though I attempted to keep a pleasurable demeanor and stray away from the bothersome comments, it was all anyone could focus on. Soon threats of hospitalizing me began and the already tiresome holiday was ruined entirely. I couldn't wait to return to my own home and retreat away into my room as I did every day. I was hardly ever home and had managed to evade being noticed that way, but this forced family time was ruining my ability to quietly slip away.

When I returned home, my father brought a scale down to the living room and asked me to stand on it. I was horrified, I hadn't weighed myself in months, I certainly wouldn't do it in front of my family. I was confident that my weight had not dropped from my own observations while looking in the mirror. I argued my way out of being weighed before going to work for the evening but now that I had been exposed, it was certainly only a matter of time before it all went downhill.

I was ambushed by a surprise doctor's appointment to weigh me not more than a week later. I felt betrayed, humiliated, and angry that nobody believed me. I hadn't lost weight; I looked the same as I always had. Eating was terrifying, but my body was used to being deprived of nutrients. I had spent years learning how to function to a reasonable extent with nothing in my system to propel me throughout my day. I wasn't focused on weight anyways, the problem laid in my thighs, hips, and chest, the parts of me I felt betrayed my masculine appearance.

The doctor took one look at the scale and suggested I attempt to drink supplement shakes throughout the day before adding, "If you're unable to gain a bit of weight, it may be time to consider hospitalization."

Chapter Seven: A Tear in the Headlights

"In order for connection to happen, we have to allow ourselves to be seen, really seen."

-Brené Brown

I trudged up the stairs to walk Bronwyn and Emilia to their next class, desperate for a few more precious moments with Bronwyn. It was pathetic and entirely out of my way, sometimes I didn't even get to talk to Bronwyn during the commute, but it was worth it to me when I could. I was quiet this time, searching for a way to bring *it* up. This idea of a plan the adults around me were forming seemed entirely dramatic and impossible, so improbable that I shouldn't even let it touch my lips. I hate surprises, I've always tried to be as transparent as possible to avoid surprising other people, and this pushed me to speak the ridiculous idea into the crowded hallway surrounding us.

"So you know how I had a doctor's appointment today?" I muttered in a nervous fluster.

"Yeah, is everything ok?" Bronwyn asked either out of politeness or concern.

"Well, they want to send me to St. Louis for my eating disorder. To a long-term facility, for months." I couldn't see any of my surroundings as I heard the words leave my mouth. Once I finished speaking, I kept my eyes on the ground, not wanting to see her reaction.

"Wait are you serious? When?" Bronwyn's voice peaked with anxiety.

"I don't know. It could be anytime, I guess. But these facilities are voluntary, I'll just say no. It really shouldn't happen, they just want it to," I tried to assure her.

"You'll be so far away," she nearly whispered as she left me to walk into her classroom.

I'll be so far away. I pushed the thought out of my mind, there was no way they were going to get me to consent to go to a facility. I wasn't even very thin in my opinion. I had probably lost a pound at the most and everyone was overreacting. I looked the same as I always had, my thighs were too large at the top, and my hips were too curvy, giving them a feminine appearance. I could see my trachea and I enjoyed it; it nearly gave me the impression of an immature Adams apple. I appreciated how pronounced my jawline was, how the harsh angles of it contoured my skin. I liked how my clothes hung from my frame, not revealing my figure. I was nearly there, if I lost just a little more weight in my thighs and hips, I would be perfect. I had always looked this way; the doctors' dramatization was going to send me hundreds of miles away from home.

I went to work that evening weighed down by anxiety. I asked Jolene to sit in my car with me for a while after our shifts and told her what I had been told. "I don't want to leave. I'm just trying my best to survive until I can medically transition, and this is the best I can do right now."

"I honestly have to agree that you need help," she replied. "Is there anything I can do to make things a little better? Maybe I could draw you pictures or something to brighten your day. I see such an amazing future for you, you really have to stay alive. Things are going to be so different soon. I've been where you are, but it truly does get better."

"Thanks, Jolene. I just don't think it will and even if it does, it will take forever for things to change," I argued.

"Maybe it will take a while, but you'll get there and it will be so glorious when you do. Please just keep going. I love you."

"I love you too," I assured her. I gave her a long hug before getting into my own car and driving home.

The next day, I went to school with the supplement drinks in a lunchbox. I quickly hid them in a locker, embarrassed to even be associated with food or eating. I gave up on school that day, knowing that soon I would no longer be attending. I stopped trying to pay attention in class and let my grades slip carelessly. I hardly looked forward to anything, even my birthday held little meaning. I put together a Christmas list full of items I had no real desire for. I was past the point of material happiness.

My self-harm became more intense and, seeing as I had run out of room on my left arm, I learned how to cut myself in a somewhat straight line with my non-dominant hand on my right arm. My lower arm quickly filled with twenty open cuts. My hand would swell up from the bandaging and the widespread pain would slow me down at work, but I continued regardless. I used toilet paper to soak up the blood and wrapped it in a black adhesive bandage. It was difficult to bandage by myself and I did everything I could to keep the wounds open, not caring for them at all.

One night at work, the pain became too much, and I decided to entrust Callie with the most vulnerable part of me. I needed help bandaging it, it was so terrible that I wasn't sure how to care for it on my own. I took her to my car during our break, making sure to warn her about what I needed help with and ask her if she would be ok.

Once she promised that she would be ok, I began to peel the hardened, blood-soaked toilet paper away from my wounds, exposing them one by one. It was incredibly painful, and I winced and squirmed in my seat as I continued pulling at it. Once it was fully off and blood began dripping from the reopened cuts, she pulled out her phone flashlight to take a better look.

"Oh my god, Faber. Oh my god," she breathed. She pointed at one, "That one is super deep, you probably need stitches on most of these."

"No way, I'll get sent to an institution" I rebuffed. "Can you please just help me put some cream on it and bandage it back up?"

"What did you even use?" she gawked.

"A pencil sharpener blade," I confessed. I pulled out a sachet of ointment I had stolen from the first aid box a few minutes prior and held it towards her, "Will this sting?"

She examined the packet, "No it won't." I began generously applying it to my arm, making a paste of blood and greasy ointment. "You're still bleeding. Here, let me get something better than toilet paper to cover that," she offered, tossing the soiled paper out the window.

She returned from her car a few seconds later with a stack of napkins she had stashed away from work. She placed them gently on my arm and I began trying to wrap it up myself. I placed my chin on the end of the bandage as I always did to hold it in place while the rest of the bandage orbited around my arm. Seeing how crude it was, she took the bandage from me and began wrapping it herself, asking me several times to tell her if she hurt me. It didn't hurt, the compression eased the stinging and transformed it into a throbbing pain instead. Afterwards, we went back to work and never brought up the experience again.

My birthday arrived quicker than I anticipated, and I was swept up into a celebration I never asked for. My choir class sang Happy Birthday to me, it was the first time I had ever heard it sung with my real name. Bronwyn made sure to remind the teacher and watched my reaction, smiling widely. Despite how miserable I was, I couldn't hide the smile that overtook my own lips and blushed timidly. My name sounded even sweeter in the form of a song, completed with harmonies only a choir could produce.

Callie had promised to spend time with me for my birthday and had insisted I took the day off work. I met her in the parking lot of our workplace and ran into her minivan. "Happy birthday, Faber!" she squealed. "I have a surprise for you." She produced a large sketchbook and a roll of art supplies from her back seat. "I didn't have time to wrap them, I hope that's ok."

I smiled, I wasn't used to being on the receiving end of platonic gift giving. "It's ok. Thank you, I love it!"

"Let's go through the drive through to see Jolene and Devyn," she suggested. I agreed and she pulled through the drive through, ordering some food for herself and announcing that I was with her to Devyn over the speaker.

We were greeted at the window by a cheery Devyn and Jolene. "Happy birthday, Faber!" they chimed.

"Faber, wait for us to go on break and we can celebrate, but first I have a gift for you!" Jolene exclaimed. She held out a small handmade paper booklet to me. "Read it now, I want to see your reaction."

I stared at the cover, embellished with stars and titled "Faber's Book of Happy" before flipping through the pages. It was filled with loving messages, hand drawn pictures, and promised that we'd be friends forever and that I was very loved. I nearly began to cry before my manager showed up at the window and shooed the girls away.

"Faber, tomorrow HR is coming in to discuss the current situation with you and Callie. You can't talk to anybody about this, do you understand? One word about it, and you're fired. It will mess up the investigation," he threatened.

The "current situation" had been steadily rising to a tipping point the previous few weeks. One of the new managers had made several people, including me, uncomfortable. I hadn't expected them to open an investigation regarding it, but I was relieved they had. Callie, Devyn, Jolene and I had truly bonded over the experience, and I was viewed as the main source of information as I had seemingly been targeted.

Callie and I promised not to tell a soul and she dropped me off at my car to wait for Devyn and Jolene's break while she went to work a shift at her other job. She asked me to join her after I finished celebrating with Devyn and Jolene and I agreed. It was completely dark outside despite it being early in the evening. I watched through my rearview mirror as two shadowy figures walked out of the building and Jolene and Devyn came into view, beckoning me to join them in Devyn's car. Her car was red, with crystals hung from the mirror and tapestries draping her messy back seats.

"We don't have a cake or candles!" Jolene realized as we got into the car.

"I have an idea," Devyn replied. "Faber, hand me that bag."

I handed her the patchwork bag sitting next to me that held all her smoking supplies. She dug around for a minute and produced a red lighter. She flicked it and a small frame began happily dancing as they sang happy birthday to me and urged me to blow it out. I did after making a wish. I didn't believe in wishes coming true anymore, but it was a longstanding tradition. I couldn't stop smiling, it was far different than my previous birthday that I had spent crying. I spent the remainder of the evening with Callie before we went back to work to help Devyn and Jolene close up and finish hanging out for the evening.

Nothing lasts forever, and the next day was just as bluntly depressing as the days leading up to my birthday. I tried to eat, I tried very hard. Every bite I took turned sour in my mouth as my brain screamed at me. I couldn't shut it up, I couldn't shut it out. I would start taking small bites of food, only to instantly regret it and spit it back out. I didn't even attempt to eat when I was around people, it was an impossible task. They were watching me, judging me, waiting to catch me in the lie that I never ate. If I never ate, I would be dead; I just ate very, very little. A few bites of food a day was the most I could convince myself to swallow.

It had always been this way, right? Surely I wasn't eating any less than before if I couldn't imagine a life of eating more. I had always been the one to engage in lunchroom conversation with empty table space in front of me, the one who hid food, the one who spit out far more food than I swallowed. It was a believable lie that I told myself, founded by several past experiences. At one point in my life, I had been able to eat so little food that I had forgotten how to swallow, and I had choked on anything I attempted to. I couldn't imagine that I had gotten worse than that, yet somehow I had, and it had all been unknowingly.

All the effort I had previously put into starving myself all boiled down to nothing. This was an effortless, uncontrollable spiral. Part of my denial came from that I believe. I was so angry that I had spent years trying to hold my hunger at bay, trying to hide it from everyone, trying to train my body to function with no sustenance, all for it to succeed once I was no longer trying. It was too easy, surely the doctors were lying to me, and I wasn't falling behind at all. It had to be some sort of trick.

A few days before Christmas, clarification stumbled upon me. I fell ill, with a sore throat, exhausted body, and burning forehead. Seeing as I had to have a doctor's note to call off work, my mom took me to the nearest Urgent Care. They ran a few tests and determined that I had contracted Strep Throat. I was pleased with the confirmation that I had a reasonable excuse to have called off work and wasn't being lazy.

Before allowing me to leave, they realized they had forgotten to weigh me and asked me to step onto the scale. They had no knowledge of my eating disorder and said nothing when I stepped on the scale facing forwards. My mom, likely out of the sudden nature of it all, also didn't correct me. I waited a few seconds until I heard the mechanical beep before looking at the electric display. Bright red numbers read, "85.5." I stared at the number in disbelief, it was ten pounds lighter than the previous time I had weighed myself. I hadn't been that weight in two years, not since the beginning of my intentional starvation. They weren't lying. I could hardly hide the shock on my face; it didn't make sense.

Christmas arrived only a few days later, I received a Walkman and a new iPod. I enjoyed collecting old technology, but I was hardly exited for the gifts. I listened to a few cassettes on the Walkman before retiring to my room for the remainder of the day to hide away. I wanted desperately for winter break to end so I could go back to school and get out of the house again. It was harder to hide the fact that I wasn't eating at home, and I still felt a lingering tension between me and my parents.

I bought Devyn, Jolene, Bronwyn, and Callie lavish Christmas gifts worth hundreds of dollars. They had been so kind to me, I felt they deserved it. I spent hours wrapping each gift intricately in brown wrapping paper before hand-drawing designs on each package. Every gift was truly beautiful, the wrapping alone was a piece of art. I got Jolene a cassette player and recorded mix tapes for her since she loved music and retro things. Devyn received a Polaroid printer that could print polaroid pictures from her phone seeing as she had a taste for visuals and aesthetics. I gifted Callie a mini fridge, skincare products, and haircare products as she loved pampering herself and had to look good to feel good. They each received their gifts in awe and gave me one in return, which I was extremely pleased with and grateful for. Bronwyn's gift hadn't arrived yet, and likely wouldn't for a few more months.

When I went into work in early January after recovering from strep throat, their attitudes towards me seemed to have shifted. Devyn and Jolene no longer greeted me and whispered without inviting me to join them. I tried to pretend I didn't notice and occasionally tried to talk to them but was ignored. I had gotten involved in a lot of drama revolving the manager making people uncomfortable and hadn't listened to their advice, but I didn't understand why that would cause them to be so cold to me. I racked my brain for anything else I could have done, the only thing I could come up with was that my mental health problems were too much for them to handle. Perhaps they didn't know how to react to my inevitable hospital stay and had instead decided to be entirely cold towards me.

No matter the reason behind it, I felt terrible every time I went to work. Callie occasionally greeted me, but even she stopped hanging out with me after work and no longer texted me. I kept my head low and stayed quiet, no longer giving them updates on the hospital situation or attempting to talk to them at all. I could understand if my problems were too heavy for someone to hold, but hadn't they asked me to talk to them when I was struggling? Hadn't they told me they cared? If that was the problem, we could have had a mature conversation, they could have at least explained to me what I did wrong.

As they say, when one door closes, another one opens. After they began to ice me out, I grew closer to Daisy once more. She had been in a similar situation before, having gone through eating disorder treatment a few years prior. She took me under her wing and cradled me, allowing me to be open with her and ask her questions about treatment. At one point, things got a bit overwhelming for her. She was able to let me know, and we talked through it. I was understanding and was more careful about what I told her from then on. We never had a problem after that and as the weeks went by, our friendship continued to bloom. She attempted to push me to eat more or drink the shakes at the very least, but ultimately respected that I couldn't.

January brought on bitterly cold weather and my favorite time of the year, Madrigal season. Madrigals was a choir event in which we held a banquet, dressed up as renaissance era characters, and sang medieval songs. I loved Madrigals more than life itself. The music was beyond heavenly, and I had already been rehearsing all year in preparation for the season. I often showed up to rehearsals with my fingers bandaged as the cold weather caused them to double in size and become extremely painful. Nevertheless, rehearsals were immersive and magical, and I looked forward to each one. The banquets were scheduled to begin on February 18, a date that remained ingrained in my memory.

Before my next weekly doctor's appointment, I made sure to hug Bronwyn goodbye just in case. Things could change in a matter of seconds; I could be sent away at any time. This wasn't our first time saying goodbye to each other in preparation, it had become a weekly event. She was far taller than me and my head fit right under her chin, like pieces of a puzzle connecting. I was willing to hug very few people but found comfort in Bronwyn's embrace. It was a sad, desperate exchange, an acknowledgement that I may not see her again for a while.

71

At the appointment, I put on the paper gown and hid my bandaged wrist behind my back as usual. The nurse came in and weighed me before instructing me to keep the gown on for the doctor to come see me. I felt the pit of my stomach drop, they were finally going to find out the extent of my self-harm. I knew there was nothing I could do to avoid it anymore and sat on the examination table waiting anxiously. I texted Bronwyn an update, telling her that things might go poorly this time.

The doctor came into the room and looked at me with a shocked expression. I was entirely exposed, the deepest part of me that I had hidden for years out in the open. She unraveled the bandages on my wrist and threw the blood-soaked toilet paper hugging my skin away in disgust before bandaging me once more. She warned me that the next time I self-harmed, I would be sent to the hospital. Then, miraculously, she let me go home. I got into my car and immediately began sobbing, the power of secrecy had been robbed from me.

I drove to the school parking lot and texted Daisy to meet me in my car after mock trial practice had ended. She came and I told her everything that had happened, not allowing myself to cry in front of her. I told her everything I had kept to myself for years, how I did it, why I did it, why I couldn't stop. We tried making light of our similar experiences, laughing a bit too boisterously over our vulnerability. We saw Bronwyn exit the building and walk to her red minivan and I begged Daisy to get her for me before she left. Daisy ran to her minivan, banging on her window and soon Bronwyn had replaced her spot in the passenger seat of my car.

"I'm sorry, Bronwyn, I'll try not to take long," I promised. "They found my self-harm. The next time I do it, they're going to send me to the hospital. That means I'm going next week. I do it every day, I can't stop."

I watched her expression darken and she refused to look me in the eyes. We talked for a while as the sky began to dim. After around half an hour, I became completely undone and admitted, "I don't know what to do. I don't know what I'm doing. I could just die, I've made it so easy for myself. I never imagined living very long. It's a good time to go."

Her hands began to shake, and I watched her fight back tears. "I think anything that keeps you alive is a good thing," she responded carefully.

"I have a rope in my car," I told her. "I spent hours braiding it to make sure it holds when I use it to hang myself. I take it with me everywhere I go, just in case. It's just been so hard, I don't know what to do."

The tears she had spent the entire interaction holding back began to flow unintentionally. They reflected the lights coming from the headlights of cars in the parking lot. It was a gut-wrenching scene. Something in the tragedy of it all assured me that she truly cared about me after all. My doubts dissipated as I watched her cry. I observed quietly, restricting my own tears to be strong for her.

"Can I give you a hug?" she asked shakily. I nodded and draped myself over her shoulders, ignoring the armrest in between us. She held me for a while as she shook and cried. I tried to provide her with some comfort, petting the strands of hair flowing down her back as we embraced. I don't think I've ever felt more guilty than I did in that moment watching her cry over me. My heart physically ached inside my rib cage as I listened to her sniffle quietly.

"Will I see you at school tomorrow?" she cried.

I thought about it for a moment before deciding, "Yes, Bronwyn. I'll be at school tomorrow, I promise."

She stayed in my car for a while longer and I was able to temporarily ease the guilt I felt by making her laugh. The rest of our conversation revolved around jokes and laughter as she regained her composure. We discussed ridiculous quotes from politicians and recounted our most embarrassing stories. The air around us lightened just enough for us to breathe again as we giggled.

I self-harmed that night, like every night before, and sealed my fate. I would certainly be going to the hospital in a week or less. I kept my promise and showed up to school but I was withdrawn and stressed. I didn't even attempt to eat or drink the supplement shakes, there was no point anymore. I decided to go to work that night, even though I wasn't scheduled to tell Callie what had happened. Even though Jolene and Devyn had been ignoring me, I held on to a thin hope that my sweet Callie still cared about me.

I showed up to work and found Callie behind the service counter. I told her the news and she seemed disappointingly apathetic. I turned to leave but was surprisingly stopped by the sound of Jolene calling my name. I walked over to where she and Devyn stood with an evil glint in their eyes and stood in front of them expectantly. Were they going to explain themselves? Perhaps they intended to apologize and let me know that they did care about me after all and they were sorry for becoming so distant.

"Faber, guess who has a new boyfriend?" Jolene started.

"You?" I guessed. Jolene had broken up with her boyfriend, Leni, recently after claiming that he was too boring, and she needed more excitement in a relationship.

"No! Daisy Kavlov!" she snarled. Daisy had told me about her new boyfriend, I guess I hadn't given it much thought with everything else going on in my life at the time. "She stole Leni! We have to destroy her, and we need you to help us."

I didn't want to help them; Daisy had been so kind to me. Jolene had broken up with Leni without warning and I didn't see a problem with him moving on and dating Daisy. My people pleasing tendencies prevailed and I decided to play the part of being willing to help if I had to, but not actually follow through with it. First, I tried to reason with them, "I have a lot going on right now guys, I'm about to go to the hospital."

"But you're our messenger!" Devyn protested. "You have to tell her to kill herself! Tell her that we hate her and she's a cunt and a slut."

I had absolutely no intention of betraying Daisy after all she had done for me, and these were messages I wouldn't have passed on to my worst enemy, but I tried to remain agreeable. "Ok, I'll try to pass the message along. I'm honestly really busy right now though, you might be on your own for this one."

"But Faber, you're like our little rat!" Jolene pleaded.

That was the final straw, I felt my heart break inside of me while the smile remained on my face. They were using me, all along they had been using me. They had stopped talking to me when I no longer served a purpose and now that I was of value again, they were willing to converse with me just enough to spread their evil plan. They had used me and no longer cared enough to even attempt to hide it. It hurt to know they thought so lowly of me that they expected me to follow their commands regardless of how I felt.

Jolene must have seen a microscopic change in my expression because she began to backpedal, "I mean... you're not a rat, but you know what I mean."

"Yeah, I get it," I said in an overly friendly tone. "I have to go guys, I'm sorry."

I cried on the way home and filled Daisy in on their plan the next day, warning her to block them on social media and ignore anything they said about her. I discussed my own stressors with her for a while and we made a pros and cons list before deciding I should text my mom and ask to go to the hospital early. After all, it was inevitable at this point, and the sooner I went, the better chance I had of being home in time to perform at madrigals. My mother's response surprised me, she told me no. She insisted that I went to see the theatre show she had bought me tickets for on my birthday before going to the hospital. It was the day before my next doctor's appointment was scheduled.

I went to the show in St. Louis after having a breakdown beforehand. I was yelled at for causing us to leave late, but I was so stressed I hardly even processed the reprimands. All I wanted was to go to the hospital and get it over with. I had to be home for Madrigals. I watched the show, it was incredible, yet I didn't find myself enjoying it. Under any other circumstances, it would have been the highlight of my year, but now it brought me minimal joy.

The day of my doctor's appointment, I left school early after hugging Bronwyn one last time. It wasn't our best goodbye hug, but I figured I'd be back in a week or two and it would suffice. My self-harm had only grown worse in the week leading up to my appointment. I hated having my privacy invaded as if I was an animal in a zoo. I felt as though if they wanted a show, I would give them one. I went to the doctor and for a moment, it seemed as though I would get lucky once more and get home.

Just as I took a breath of relief, the doctor said, "Go home and pack for the hospital."

Chapter Eight: The Graphite Window

"I can go anywhere I want, anywhere I want just not home."

– Taylor Swift

The lights of the city illuminated the night as we drove quietly. We arrived at the Children's Hospital after several wrong turns. The hospital was only thirty minutes away from my home, which didn't seem terribly far away. I grabbed my pillow and suitcase and followed my mom to the walkway leading from the parking garage to the main floor of the hospital. We found the admittance desk and had our pictures taken. My mom was given a badge to allow her to leave and return as she pleased.

The hospital was large and I was excited to be able to wander around it as it was a hospital only for children this time. I had been admitted to general pediatrics, not an eating disorder or psychiatric ward, and assumed I wouldn't be confined to a single floor this time. We went up the elevator and walked down the light yellow hallway through the locked doors leading to my section of the hospital. I was placed in room 623, a decently large room with a TV, tables, a desk, a bed, a bathroom, and a long couch sitting underneath the vast window covering an entire wall of the room.

My mother left soon after the nurses had checked me in and given me a blue gown to change into. A nurse sat outside of my door, monitoring me. I was uncomfortable with this and tried to ignore her as I texted my friends updates. The silence quickly became harsh and drawn out and I mumbled, "I miss my friends already and I just got here."

"Me too, buddy," she replied. "I'm usually an ER nurse. I don't really know what I'm doing up here, they just told me to sit here and watch you."

We talked about my friends for a while before more nurses came in to place an IV in the crook of my arm. The nurse sitting outside my door was eager to help and insisted she could do it, but they didn't let her. It was clear that the change of pace from her typical work environment was boring her. The IV didn't hurt, I only felt a small pinch before they began drawing blood out of it. I had to have my blood drawn every four hours to ensure I didn't get refeeding syndrome from the sudden increase in my food intake.

I didn't eat for the entire first evening, I just talked to the nurse outside my door and allowed others to poke and prod at me endlessly. They decided I needed to take a vitamin pill and I protested that it was much too large to swallow. The nurse who was assigned to watch me took out a plastic pill crusher and crushed it into a fine powder before pouring it on top of cup of applesauce. She didn't mix it in, knowing I wouldn't want to have to eat the entire cup. She walked up to me and fed me the applesauce and pill powder in three spoonfuls, lifting each one to my mouth as if I were a small child. It could have been instinctual from her time spent in the ER, but I felt cared for and labeled her as a new mother figure.

Doctors and nurses assessed the wounds on my arm and decided they may need stitches. They scheduled a consultation for me and left as quickly as they had come in. I told the nurse assigned to me, I never caught her name, all about my friends and madrigals and work drama. We laughed together and had an entertaining conversation before she suggested I try to sleep. I wasn't particularly tired, but she convinced me to attempt to stick to my sleeping schedule to make the transition back to school go smoother. Remembering that I was going back to school gave me hope and I clung to it like a spider hanging from a thin strand of webbing.

Throughout the night, I was woken up several times to have my vitals taken and my blood drawn. The monitor next to my bed kept beeping loudly when my heart rate slowed in my sleep and a newborn baby cried in the room next to me. These factors combined allowed me to get next to no sleep despite my best efforts. When I was woken up once again to have my blood drawn around 4:00 a.m., I finally sat up and admitted defeat. I pulled out my AirPods and listened to music for a while until the morning nurses came in to introduce themselves and weigh me. I had to turn around to face away from the display while I waited to hear the beep alerting me that it was finished calculating my weight. They referred to this as a "blind weight," a standard protocol for eating disorder patients.

I met with an array of doctors and nurses who filtered in and out of my room at random intervals. My nurses' names that day were Wren and Carrie, and my dietician's name was Brianna. I didn't pay attention to my doctors' names, there were far too many of them traveling in a pack. I was put on complete bedrest, I was only allowed to stand up to go to the bathroom when being supervised by a nurse and showers were limited to five minutes. My room was above the helicopter landing pad, and I tried to pass the time by watching the helicopters come and leave. They were so loud that my room shook a bit upon each return.

A surgeon came in to assess the most recent wounds on my arm and decided it was too late for stitches. The wounds were too far along in the healing process and couldn't be grafted together properly. She rinsed them with a gentle solution made for babies in the NICU and covered them with an absorbent pad before sliding a mesh sleeve on top of everything to hold it all together. With the white bandages covering my arm, wires coming out of my chest, an IV in my arm, and a pulse sticker taped to my finger, I looked like Dear Evan Hanson gone terribly wrong.

The nurses discovered I could easily fit into the pediatric hospital uniforms rather than the tragically oversized gown I was wearing and provided me with soft shorts and a shirt that was tied in the back. The shorts relieved the dysphoria the gown had given me, and I was grateful to have a fraction of my misery taken from me. Wren and Carrie were wonderful nurses, they came into my room to talk to me when they weren't busy to prevent me from getting too lonely. We talked about the drag shows they were planning on attending and the madrigals I was so desperate to participate in.

I spent hours scrolling mindlessly through my phone until I began to realize something. My friend Kenneth had been in the hospital for weeks, undergoing chemotherapy, and the hospital walls in his

79

photos were the same color as the walls in my room. I texted him and asked which hospital he was in, and it turned out we were in the same place. I excitedly began asking if we could plan a time to hang out while we were both there, and he agreed to meet with me the next day.

I technically still wasn't allowed to walk, but the nurses allowed me to walk to the game room with him only once. He met me at my door and I followed him to the game room slowly, being in bed for so long had sent my head spinning when I tried to walk. He was in regular street clothes but pulled an IV pole delivering fluids to him along with him as he walked. My own IV had stopped returning blood and the constant needle sticks had left the back of my hands and inner arms badly bruised. All of my veins had blown, and though I didn't have any distaste for needles, the constant poking had become more painful now that I was severely bruised.

We sat in the game room, but quickly realized that we would rather talk than play anything. I had been forbidden from playing air hockey as it "burned too many calories," and that was the only game that appealed to us. We talked about choir and madrigals and school and how long we expected to be in the hospital. I got to meet his mother who was staying with him, but after a brief conversation, she left the two of us alone again. We talked about our favorite nurses and how lonely it was to be in the hospital sometimes.

It was so nice to talk to somebody who understood. Somebody who was also unexpectedly ripped away from everything they knew and didn't know when things would go back to normal again. Of course, our circumstances were very different, but they were simultaneously eerily similar. We tried to make the best of our situations, he told me to put fairy lights up in my room to make it more like home. I texted my mom immediately, asking her to buy fairy lights. Everyone needs a little brightness in their darkest times, even if it's artificial.

The next day, my mom and I hung up the fairy lights in between blood tests and vitals checks. They were cheery and bright and traced the doorways, illuminating the figure of Jesus on a cross hung on the wall. The hospital was a Christian organization and often recited prayers over the loudspeaker or invited people to attend Sunday Mass. It was strange to me as I hadn't been in a Christian setting in quite some time. I felt that God, if he existed, should mind his own business and stay out of my miserable life. The last place I wanted to hear a prayer was in my hospital bed miles away from everyone I loved.

Bronwyn sent me daily pictures to cheer me up. I always smiled at them and showed them off to my nurses when they came in to talk to me or run another test. She made it her goal to send me a picture every day after hearing that it made me smile. Typically, she was posed with the entirety of the choir class, all with beaming faces and poses holding up hearts or peace signs. Very few of them knew where I was, I had only told my closest friends and had given stern instructions not to tell anyone who wasn't already aware.

I don't remember much of my time in the hospital. I recall drawing with the nurses, spending hours making bracelets with minuscule beads to give to my friends, and making them cards and gift baskets for Valentines Day. I went a bit stir crazy after an entire week of bed rest and not being able to see the halls, but I felt much better after seeing Kenneth. He had chemotherapy the day afterwards and was ill for the remainder of my stay, so we didn't have the opportunity to see each other again. I wish I could recollect more, but the days were long and washed out in my mind with very little to distinguish one day from the previous or the next.

I drew a picture of the window looking out into the city with pencils from my bed and the nurses showed it off to each other proudly. Above it I wrote the quote, "I can go anywhere I want, anywhere I want, just not home," by Taylor Swift to describe my circumstances. I received no gifts or letters from my friends, but I was bought two piglet stuffed animals by my parents and was given a few other stuffed animals by charities visiting the hospital. One was a dog half my size with a puppy attached to it which I hugged like a friend and cried on often.

On my seventeenth day of my hospital stay, they informed me that I was not allowed to go home. I would be sent to an eating disorder facility long term, a residential facility. They reported that they were searching for openings for me and while the treatment was "voluntary" and I was allowed to turn opportunities down, I would remain in the hospital until I agreed to treatment and had secured a spot in a facility. I was absolutely shocked, I had known that treatment relied on consent, so I had planned on simply not agreeing, but the choice had been taken from me. I had to consent, or I would never leave.

A few hours later, my dietician rushed into the room to tell me that a bed had opened up at a facility in Saint Louis called Pomegranate. Several doctors, nurses, and social workers flooded into my room to encourage me to agree to go before giving me five minutes to make a choice. They agreed to allow me to keep some of the hospital clothes if I went, seeing as I was so comfortable in them. I didn't want to go. It was three hours away from my home and I was certain my friends would never visit. Beyond that, I was now going to miss madrigals and possibly the rest of my school year. It was a body stiffening decision to make.

I drew out the decision for as long as I could before the time ran out and I decided, "Ok, I'll go."

Chapter Nine: A New Home

" 'I'll take care of you.' 'It's rotten work.' 'Not to me, not if it's you.' "

-Anne Carson

I was allowed to go home briefly to collect my things. While I was there, I found a small blade I had hidden in my room and used it to cut into my thigh. When I had finished and wrapped my thigh up neatly, I wrapped the blade in toilet paper to keep it from rattling or jingling and stuffed it inside of a floss container I put in my lilac toiletry bag. I hoped it was clever enough to bypass any bag checks they performed when I got to the facility.

I stepped back into the van anxiously and my dad handed me an envelope, "Here's the pictures you sent me, they all came out bad."

I opened the envelope as the van began cruising through our neighborhood. The pictures were terribly pixilated, I could hardly make out my friends' faces. Tears filled my eyes and a lump swelled in my throat. "Can we reprint them please? I really need these pictures." I choked out.

My dad shook his head and explained we had to be at the facility by 5:00 p.m. and we had a three-hour drive ahead of us to Missouri. I began to cry uncontrollably, Bronwyn's pictures helped me get through my stay at the hospital, I couldn't do this without her even if she was only formed by pixels on a sheet of glossy paper. Tears continued to stream down my face as I texted my friends to explain that I wouldn't have access to my phone for a while. Emilia sent a final photo of her and Bronwyn to cheer me up after hearing that I was upset. I smiled a bit upon seeing their faces. I could see a quiet sadness on Bronwyn's face despite her forced smile but looked past it and was able to stop crying for the remainder of the drive.

Eventually, a winding road took us to a vast brick house. Copper accented the enormous roof and chimneys, the driveway had been converted into a small parking lot that comfortably accommodated our van. I took out my AirPods and housed them in their case, ceasing the loop of "Seven" by Taylor Swift serving as the score to our journey. I grabbed my backpack and pillow and trudged behind my parents to the door of the house.

A pink stained glass rose complimented the ornate wooden door I stood face to face with. A tanned woman with black hair and striking blue eyes opened the door and let us in and we were quickly ushered into a side room. My parents sat on the long couch and I sat across from them in an armchair adjacent to the fireplace. I anxiously tapped my foot until a tall blonde woman led us into another room connected by a door to the room we sat in.

The new room, called "the Family Room," was brighter, a baby blue hexagonal room with sunlight pouring in through the windows and white accents. The woman, who introduced herself as Caprese, talked to my parents about the routines and policies of the residential facility. I tuned her out, staying silent when she looked towards me for a response. I was too distraught to talk, to listen, to be amicable. My parents and I signed countless forms, despite already signing several during our drive. Eventually, Caprese left us alone to say our goodbyes. I quietly and swiftly bid my parents goodbye before following Caprese down the narrow hallway to the door leading to the other room.

As my parents left, I was pleased to see other children. I hadn't seen kids my age in weeks besides Kenneth, but four children sat at the dining room table across from me with two adults. Olivia Rodrigo music played on a Bluetooth speaker as they rhythmically ate the food on their plates. I started to walk towards the table, but was interrupted by another adult, a gentle looking woman with deep brown eyes and long black hair. She led me past the table, the massive orange couch in the living room which she called "the milieu," the kitchen, and into another hallway tucked behind the rest of the house.

"I'm Chealsea, one of the nurses here," she explained as we walked. "I'm going to need to do a skin check, and a basic questionnaire. Your dinner is in the room we'll be in already." She opened a white door in the middle of the hallway to our right and followed me inside.

I shifted nervously; I didn't expect to make this confession so soon upon my arrival. "I self-harmed," I admitted quietly, keeping my eyes on the sandwich sitting on a plate waiting for me. Chelsea's expression remained placid and I began removing my clothes as she instructed me to, leaving my pants for last. Finally, I took off my jeans and began to unravel the bandage hugging my thigh.

Blood began dripping down my leg and Chelsea cleaned it with a wet gauze pad before taking pictures of the self-inflicted wounds. "This one might need stitches," she muttered as she pointed at the deepest gash. She wrapped my thigh in clean bandages and began asking me questions after I put my clothes back on. I ate my sandwich slowly, taking breaks to answer the endless questionnaire questions. Finally, I had provided enough adequate answers to leave the room and join the other children who were now watching a movie in the milieu.

I sat in the middle section of the orange fabric couch, a brunette girl sat to the left of me, a blonde girl and a lighter brunette girl sat to the right of me, and a brown-haired boy sat in a swivel chair behind the couch. For a few minutes there was an awkward silence among us as actors danced across the TV screen. Finally, the boy asked, "What's your name?"

"Faber," I nearly whispered. "What are your names?" I asked slightly louder.

"I'm Taylor," the girl to the left of me responded. Her voice was soothing and gentle, her long dark brown hair and eyes reminded me of Bronwyn, and I felt immediately connected to her.

"I'm Brock," the boy in the chair answered between short fits of burps. "I heard that you're seventeen like the rest of the kids here, but you look my age and I'm thirteen."

"Be quiet, Brock," the other brunette girl spat. "My name is Marianna by the way. And that's Rachel," she added, pointing to the blonde girl. "She's a little shy but super sweet."

Everyone's attention redirected to the television screen as Brock began to ramble about the movie and actors. I responded carelessly as I carefully observed everyone around me. Nobody looked particularly happy, but they didn't seem miserable either. Perhaps the facility was as grand as the house that hosts it, and I had no reason to be upset to be there. I tried to relax my stiffened body, but my anxiety didn't allow me to.

The adult watching over us came around and gave each of us a plate filled with a large pretzel. I hadn't eaten in front of people my age in years. I watched everyone else slowly pick away at their pretzels and robotically fell into their rhythm. I shook as I ate it, riddled with the fear of judgement, but eventually finished it. The movie continued to play for what felt like an eternity. I didn't enjoy a single second of it, but I was grateful that it provided a distraction.

At last, the movie ended, and the adult unlocked the doors to our rooms to allow us to get ready for bed. I had my own room on the first floor next to Brock's room. The room was large and built to accommodate two people, two beds awaited tired bodies, two dressers prepared to hold clothes, two nightstands stood ready to collect trinkets. A wall of windows stood opposite the door overlooking a small collection of trees and the Mississippi River that lay beyond them from three stories high. I walked into the now unlocked bathroom and marveled at the open space and large shower as I changed into my pajamas and brushed my teeth. How could a person be so lucky and misfortuned simultaneously?

Once I finished preparing for bed, I walked to the milieu with my toothbrush in hand to be locked up in the "sharps closet." Due to my history of self-harm, I had been put on safety observations and wasn't allowed to sleep in my room. The room was locked back up and I was taken back to the nurse's station where a small blue cot sat in the hallway waiting for me. I tucked myself in and attempted to block out the light shining from inside the nurse's station as I struggled to fall asleep. The cot was no better than the hospital bed I had spent the last eighteen nights sleeping on, I yearned for my comfortable bed at home.

The next morning, I was woken up at 7:00 a.m., an hour later than the scheduled wake up time since it was Saturday. One by one, Brock, Marianna, Rachel, and Taylor entered the hallway and lined up beside my cot. I joined the line nervously, "Why are we lining up?"

"Oh, it's just for vitals. We take vitals first thing in the morning every day and on Mondays, Wednesdays, and Fridays you get weighed and have to wear your weight shirt." Taylor explained.

"My weight shirt?" I asked quietly.

"The big black t-shirt they gave you when you got here. When you get weighed, you can only wear that and your underwear," she replied.

I was relieved that I didn't have to stand there in my underwear yet, but my relief didn't last long. I had been put on daily skin checks, meaning I had to pull down my pants for the nurses to check for self-harm anyways. After my skin check, a pulse oximeter was placed on my finger while my blood pressure and temperature were taken. The vitals were taken in a small, crowded room by the nurse's station that hosted a bench, shelves full of toiletries and medical supplies, and a large scale looming in the corner.

Once Chelsea finished, I walked through the milieu to the sharps closet where I was handed the lilac fabric bag housing my toothbrush, comb, and other hygiene items by the tech, Clara. Getting ready in the mornings and getting ready for bed was the only time we were allowed to be on our own in the bathroom without someone standing outside the door. Once I was in my bathroom with the door mostly closed behind me, I opened up my floss container and took out the blade I had stashed inside.

Now that I knew the procedures, I knew they wouldn't check the part of my side hidden by my underwear during skin checks. I cut myself as I showered, allowing the flowing water to wash away the blood. The tiles I stood on became a shifting maroon watercolor display as I sliced deeper and deeper. When I finished, I grabbed a tissue from the box on the sink and held it to my side as I stepped out of the shower. I let the water continue to run as I pulled my underwear over the tissue to keep it in place and placed the blade back in the floss container.

With a newfound sense of control, I finished getting dressed, turned off the shower, and joined Brock, Rachel, and Taylor on the couch in the milieu. Clara locked my room back up for the day and began making loud animal noises to beckon Marianna to come downstairs for breakfast. We all stared up at the balcony waiting for her to appear in the doorway of her room. Finally, after Clara hollered, "Bark, bark!" in a valley girl accent, Marianna joined us downstairs and we walked to the kitchen to prepare breakfast.

Marianna, Taylor, and Rachel were on portioning, meaning they were allowed to put on hairnets and gloves and portion their own food with supervision while Brock and I sat at a small round table watching Clara portion our food. Saturday's breakfast was a cereal of our choice and some fruit, I chose Cinnamon Toast Crunch with a banana. The portion seemed completely unreasonable to me, half a bowl of cereal. I was used to eating only a small handful of cereal as my only meal of the day. I didn't finish breakfast and as per protocol was offered a shake to supplement the remainder of the meal in a tall opaque glass the other kids referred to as a "suppy cup."

The day was filled with group therapy sessions broken up by watching TV and arguing over what show to watch. Since it was Saturday, there was a group outing planned, a trip to Build-a-Bear. I wasn't allowed to go since I was new and outing privileges had to be earned. I was left in the milieu with Reya, a modelesque therapist with the complexion of an iced coffee with a bit of cream. Her appearance was intimidating, she looked as though she belonged in a group of posh judgmental celebrities, but she was as gentle as a butterfly and as sweet as honeysuckle. Her presence was serene and balanced, and I instantly felt she was going to be a source of stability and comfort for me.

88

Taylor became my closest companion at the facility quickly, she was eager to help me and explain things to me and had the gentlest soul. We ate six times a day, three meals and three snacks. Breakfast at 7:00, 8:00 on the weekends, a snack at 10:15, lunch at 12:15, a snack at 3:15, dinner at 6:00, and a final snack at 8:30. It was difficult to tolerate as the portions were much larger than at the hospital. Each meal was timed, we had to complete breakfast, lunch, and dinner within 30 minutes and snacks within fifteen minutes.

On my first Tuesday at Pomegranate, I was allowed to go on my first Tuesday meal outing. As a group, we decided to go to the food court at the mall. We drove in a large van with Clara, another tech named Raven, and the dietician, Lauren. The van was crowded, and Brock made sure the ride was noisy. I sat in the front row between Clara and Taylor as Brock poked at our heads from behind us and Marianna and Rachel attempted to stop him.

We arrived at the mall after a relatively short drive, and I was in awe of how large it was. The mall near my house was fairly small and rundown, but this mall had a multi-level parking deck attached to it. We parked on the top level and walked into Dick's. I stayed close to Taylor the entire time. I knew she was going home soon since it was nearly her 18th birthday, but I wanted to soak in her comfort as long as she was around.

We made our way to the food court and split up, keeping one adult with each group. Lauren had to approve any meal we chose and there were a lot of rules, no kids meals, no diet drinks, etc. I was with Raven and I looked into her eyes nervously, "I haven't eaten at a restaurant in years, I'm scared. I don't want to get anything."

She encouraged me to get a meal and at least try so I settled on chicken nuggets from Chick-Fil-A. I struggled to eat any of it, but ended up eating a few chicken nuggets and fries and drinking my juice box. Afterwards, I was rewarded with a trip to Build-A-Bear. I chose the same bear Taylor got, a brown sherpa bear that I affectionately named Pom after the Pomegranate facility. I carried Pom throughout the mall as Brock walked around with an ice cream cone in hand. He had such a distinct walk, I nearly giggled every time I looked at him.

I became attached to three techs within the first week, Clara, Raven, and Kayliegh, all of whom were twenty-three years old. Clara was a funny, boisterous, witty tech with straight, dyed auburn hair, and icy blue eyes. We made inside jokes and learned sign language together in our spare time, primarily curse words. Raven had light brunette hair, brown doe eyes and dimples, she was innocent and strict yet gentle. Kayliegh had fine brown hair and glasses. She was a mother and every bit as caring and comforting as one which is what drew me to her. I also became attached to two therapists, Reya and the family therapy Kendall, who we lovingly referred to as KV since there was another therapist named Cendall at the facility. KV was loud, funny, and creative, she often made signs to decorate our living space and led crafts to entertain us.

Slowly, my newfound friends began to go home. After only four days together, my closest friend Taylor graduated from the program and left. The graduation ceremony involved all the staff and kids filling the milieu and passing around a bracelet made of crystal beads. Each person assigned the graduate a word to take with them once handed the bracelet. I gave Taylor the word "helpful." "In only four days, I feel like I've known you forever. You've been so helpful to me and you're the kindest soul. I hope you can show yourself a bit of the kindness and helpfulness you've shown me as you move on to the next chapter of your life," I explained.

Once the bracelet had been passed around, it was given to the graduate to keep. We then went to a small corner next to the dining table and the door to the garage where a large painting of a tree hung. The graduate got to paint their hands or fingers in orange paint and leave a handprint or fingerprints on the tree with their initials so they would be remembered in the facility forever. Taylor made a small orange heart with two thumbprints. After the ceremony, we were allowed to hug each other for the first and only time and the graduate could hug the staff to bid them goodbye as well.

After Taylor left, I was lost for a few days. I had nobody to sit next to at meals or do "buddy bites" with. I adjusted quickly, but to my dismay my friends continued to leave. Only a few weeks later, Marianna was the next to graduate and leave. A week after that, Rachel left in the quiet fashion I expected of her. I waited for the promise of new friends, but nobody came to replace those who left. It was only Brock and I.

The day before Rachel's departure, I was finally able to get ahold of Daisy on the phone. I had been calling her and Bronwyn every day during our scheduled ten-minute phone times.

"Hey, Stink! How are you?" she cooed.

"Really bad. I'm so lonely here," I admitted.

"Well at least you're safe," she assured me. "At least you aren't hurting yourself anymore."

I let the silence linger a second too long before replying, "I still am. It's even worse than it was at home, and I don't know how to tell anyone."

Her voice darkened, "You have to tell someone. You have to."

"I know but I'm scared of what will happen if I lose it. I really don't know what to do." I coiled the phone cord around my finger and looked out the glass door of the phone room to ensure nobody could hear my whisper.

"What do you even use there?" Daisy asked.

"I snuck something in," I replied hesitantly.

"Faber!" she practically yelled back.

"I know, I know. I was just scared of losing it, it's the one thing I really need. I really need it," I pleaded. "How about I tell them and just lie about what I used?"

91

A knock on the door alerted me that my time was up as she responded, "Fine, but swear you'll tell them as soon as you get off the phone."

"I swear," I vowed. "I have to go now, I love you."

"Love you too, Stink."

And with that, I hung up the phone. I walked back to the milieu where Kayliegh sat working on a puzzle. I asked to go to the bathroom to get ready for bed and closed the door behind me. I self-harmed again, hoping it wouldn't be the last time. It was messy, blood dripped down my legs and formed sizable puddles on the floor. I wadded up a piece of toilet paper and put it under the side of my underwear to control the bleeding. I taped the blade back to the back of the toilet using a strip of the deodorant label to hide it better.

I started to clean up the mess I made but the nurse began yelling for me to hurry up and take my medications. I laid a pile of the old blood-soaked jeans and underwear in front of the largest blood puddle, shielding it from view of the doorway. I crumpled up the bloody paper towels I had wiped part of the floor with and buried them at the bottom of the trash can. Then I took a purple-colored pencil I had hidden in my sock and shoved the wooden tip into a still bleeding wound. I turned it around until the entire tip was saturated with blood and laid it on the sink to set the stage.

I went to take my meds and get my skin checked, knowing they wouldn't figure out what I'd done. The nurse pointed out a trail of dry blood on my leg, I told her I had picked on an old scab, and she accepted my explanation. I took my medications quietly and went back to the milieu thinking of the promise I had made to Daisy. Kayleigh sat quietly with her puzzle, I scooped up Pom and began to pace.

"Is something wrong, kid?" Kayleigh asked, adjusting her glasses slightly and refocusing on her puzzle.

I hesitated, I wanted to tell Kayleigh everything. I imagined her holding me, rocking me like a small child, as I cried on her shoulder. Not everything can be as you wish it to be. "I promised my friend I would tell you something, but I don't want to. Stupid promises."

Kayleigh didn't investigate further and after a while of pacing, I settled down on the couch across from her. I studied her face, anticipating her reaction, preparing myself for it. "I self harmed."

Her eyes snapped to attention, focusing on me. "When? Where?"

"Kind of since I got here. There's a bit of a mess in the bathroom right now but I don't want to show you yet, can we just talk for now? And please don't tell Nurse Tina, she's so scary, I'd rather wait and tell the night nurse," I explained in a lowered voice.

"Why did you do it? What did you use?" she asked urgently.

"I need it, I couldn't stop. It's all I have, I need it like I need water. I used a pencil," I began to lie. "I can show you where it is."

We talked for a while and once both of us were calm enough, Kayleigh got up and motioned for me to lead her to the bathroom. I walked in front of her slowly, hoping to never reach the destination. When we inevitably got to the bathroom, I opened the door and headed for the pile of clothes. I picked them up, staining my hands crimson, "They're a little bloody."

Kayliegh stood at the doorway, her eyes wide. I avoided her gaze as she gently responded, "Oh, honey..."

The puddles of blood were no longer hidden. I tossed the clothes in the laundry hamper, soiling the white mesh it was constructed of. "I cleaned up half of it, I just didn't have time to clean up the rest."

"This is half of it?" Kayleigh asked incredulously, staring at the scene.

93

"It's really not that bad," I pleaded. It was an utterly heinous sight, the blood had managed to cover nearly all of the white tile with droplets spreading to every corner, but her reaction made me wish I hadn't told her. I could hear genuine concern in her voice, something that I hadn't expected to hurt so thoroughly. *She actually cares.* I looked into her pained eyes for a second as I stood in the middle of the bathroom defeatedly.

She took a few pictures for her incident report before ushering me to Nurse Tina. "Faber has something to tell you."

"I don't want to," I whispered with my head buried in Pom's fur. "Please don't leave me," I begged Kayleigh.

"Trust me, nobody's leaving you now," Kayleigh assured me. The idea was so comforting, nobody would leave me ever again. Of course, that isn't what she meant, but I preferred to believe my interpretation of the promise. Stupid promises.

"I self harmed," I finally admitted quietly.

"Let me see," Nurse Tina puffed impatiently.

With Kayleigh's eyes trained on the hip I reached for, I pulled down the side of my pants and peeled the wadded paper from my skin, revealing my entirely sliced up side. There was less skin than tissue visible, over twenty fresh cuts covered the area. The most recent ones still dripped with blood.

Nurse Tina stood in shock, "All this happened while you were here?"

"Yes," I responded quietly.

She took several pictures of my side before throwing away the bloody pencil Kayliegh handed her. I was taken into the vitals room and bandaged. I nearly cried from sheer embarrassment when they pulled my pants slightly too far down. Dysphoria overtook me, I hadn't expected to see that region of myself in that moment and a spinning plagued my head. Eventually, my pants were pulled back up and I was allowed to sleep, this time with Nurse Tina and Kayleigh watching over my cot in the hallway.

The next morning, I went into the shower and cut myself once more after hiding away another pencil to blame. They didn't find out until the evening and seemed to still believe my story about the pencil though they questioned it a bit. I retorted that I had a technique and was able to tear myself up with anything even remotely pointy. They seemed a bit unsure, but let it slide. They added talking in the bathroom and during my shower to my safety plan, as if I couldn't talk and cut myself at the same time. I wasn't allowed to leave to go on outings anymore either, and had to watch the other kids go while I stayed behind.

The following day, I cut once more in the shower while talking to Clara who sat outside the bathroom door. I stuck a piece of toilet paper onto the gash as I got dressed and cleaned the blood off of the shower floor, burying the paper towels I used in the bottom of the trashcan. I didn't have a pencil stashed away this time, so I grabbed my rat-tailed comb and rolled the end of it on the bloody toilet paper stuck to my side. I laid it on the sink and hung up my towel that was already full of blood stains from previous incidents.

I opened the door and handed Clara my toiletry bag as she grabbed the comb before I could put it away. I had meant to pick up the comb myself, seeing as it was now a biohazard, but it was already too late. Clara began to walk towards the door leading into the milieu, but I hesitated. They were going to find out eventually anyways now that they knew where to check, and I would rather have confessed to Clara than Nurse Tina that evening. Clara paused and looked back at me, waiting for me to follow her. I stayed in place.

"Clara," I started nervously. "I self-harmed again, with the comb."

"I knew it!" she groaned. "That's why I grabbed it so quickly."

95

"It isn't that bad," I compromised, pulling back the toilet paper so she could see. My interpretation of "not that bad" was anything that didn't put me at immediate risk of bleeding to death. It was still deep and exposed layers of tissues and the purple walls of my veins.

She took me back to see the nurse and on our way, Brock began to whine. "Why does he get all the special attention?"

Clara rolled her eyes as she finished escorting me to get bandaged up. The rest of the day passed uneventfully, we had more therapy, our six timed and scheduled meals, did a bit of karaoke, and watched TV. I wasn't able to finish all of my food and downed a few supplement drinks throughout the day. Brock made some hilarious comments that only a thirteen-year-old boy was capable of making, including announcing at the breakfast table, "I know where the clitoris is!" Causing Clara and I to nearly choke on our food due to a mixture of shock and laughter.

The next morning, Raven was working and I went through my morning routine as usual but this time, I got a bit carried away. In a sudden lapse of judgement, I carved a four inch long, quarter of an inch wide laceration above the rest of the wounds covering my side. It immediately began bleeding severely, covering the shower floor in a crimson dye and running down my legs. I snapped back to reality just in time to realize how badly I had messed up. It was clear, even to me, that I had gone too far.

I scrambled to grab tissues to stuff into the gash while I got dressed and cleaned the shower. The tissues needed constant replacement as they were nearly instantly soaked through. I opened the door as soon as I was dressed and the scene was no longer traumatizing. "Raven, I went too far, it's really bad this time."

She looked up at me with her lips curled in shock. I ran to the bathroom to grab more tissues as I began to feel a sticky warmth touch my skin. Raven watched as I produced a bloody wad of tissues and stuffed fresh ones into my pants, allowing the waistband to hold them in place. I was panicking. In three years of consistently carrying out this type of self-mutilation, I had never been in a space of pure panic.

We practically ran to the nurse's station where the nurse taped several gauze pads onto my side until the padding was about an inch thick. We sat down for breakfast with Brock, and allowed him to fill the silence, which wasn't a difficult task for him. Only a few minutes had passed before I stood up to point to the blood that was beginning to seep through my shirt at an angle that only allowed Raven to see what I was referencing. She motioned for me to go back to the nurse's station. I was taped up again with an even thicker layer of gauze.

A few hours continued on in this fashion until the nurse's trash can was entirely filled with soaked gauze pads. Finally I sighed, "I think it needs stitches."

They called an Uber to transport Raven and I to the local Urgent Care. I tried to keep the mood light by commenting on the sky, clouds, and buildings. The driver was quiet and didn't question where we were going nor where we came from. Soon Raven was on the phone, and I pretended not to eavesdrop. I couldn't hear the person on the other end of the line, so the attempt was futile. I stared at the road as it flew by, watching the yellow dashed lines blur into a long, solid strip.

"I'm so sorry but we need to go back," Raven alerted the driver once she hung up. I was confused and looked at her. "They said no stitches today," she muttered to me.

We turned around and headed back, returning quicker than I expected to. When I walked in, several people remarked how quickly I came back, and I reported that we hadn't even gone to Urgent Care. Everyone seemed equally as confused. If there was ever an occasion for stitches, this was unquestionably the occasion. I had a firm belief, reinforced by my years of experience, that anything would eventually heal on its own with time and medical intervention for grazes was generally unnecessary, but even I questioned if this cut would ever be able to fuse into a scar on its own.

Nurse Tina called me back to her office and remarked, "That was a nice escape attempt. Do you really want to leave that badly?"

I hadn't even thought about leaving. I had expected to walk in, get stitches, and come back. Besides, I felt undeniably supported at Pomegranate, I enjoyed living there more than my own house. Why would I try to escape?

"I wasn't trying to escape," I defended myself. "Why would I do that? It's not like I would be going home. If anything, I would be placed in another facility. I like it here; I want to stay."

She gave me a skeptical look and asked if I had any more urges before sending me back to the milieu where Raven sat reading on her Kindle. One day, I wanted to be just like Raven, the perfect balance of caring, kind, driven, smart, and funny. I wanted to be a safe space for a kid who needed one, someone who they could always come to, someone they would look forward to seeing. I wanted to work diligently and hardly break a sweat to encourage others to be the best version of themselves. Today was not that day, tomorrow wouldn't be either, but maybe at some point in the distant future, I could be a role model for those in need.

The next day, I woke up to find the gaping gash still bleeding. I went into the shower, this time with an inflated sense of power. If that didn't need stitches, absolutely nothing would, and therefore I could get away with anything. I made two rugged slices on my side. They weren't long, but they were deep and wide, shaped like the outline of a canoe rather than a straight line. I got dressed and cleaned up the shower before announcing what I had done to Clara almost carelessly while brushing my teeth.

I ate my breakfast with Clara, Brock, and another tech named Andrea, and went down to school which was held in the second basement. We only had two hours of scheduled school time a day, which wasn't terribly drawn out. Even though I didn't enjoy it, I tried to keep my complaints minimal and be productive.

I had just begun doing work when Chealsea peered over the railing of the staircase and called for me to come upstairs. When I did, I was met with Kendell who was equipped with plastic gloves. Chelsea explained that they were going to take a look at my side and give me new bandages. I knew deep within me that this was going to shock Kendell as she had never seen my self-harm in its fresh state and immediately began to do damage control.

"It's really not that bad," I argued to her.

"Anything is bad, Faber," she replied flatly.

I was taken into the vitals room where they took more pictures of my side, this time holding a tape measure up for reference. Kendell had gone a bit pale but was able to keep her composer while the bandages were replaced. I walked back down to the schoolroom and met Clara's eyes which possessed the same nervous look as mine. Andrea and Brock pretended not to notice my entrance and remained absorbed in their activities.

Brock snapped the pen holder clip off of his mechanical pencil and I swiped it off the table before anyone noticed, hiding it in my balled-up fist. I placed my teddy bear in a position on my lap that shielded my hands from view and began scratching the top of my hand with the slightly sharp shard of plastic. Something was going on, I could feel it, and the scratching helped relieve my stress. As Clara began leaving the room for a few minutes at a time only to return later and leave once more, I began to question the invincibility that I had felt earlier that morning. I was called upstairs once more, leaving Brock and Andrea alone in the schoolroom.

Kendell stood at the top of the stairs and said, "We're calling an ambulance for you."

Chapter Ten: Jesus Take the Wheel

"Stories have to be told or they die, and when they die, we can't remember who we are or why we're here."

-Sue Monk Kidd

I sat in the middle of the orange fabric couch with Clara close beside me, shifting anxiously. A police escort had an awkward conversation with her while I clutched my teddy bear. I hardly had time to be embarrassed by the red velvet pajama pants I wore. My hand burned under the gauze Chelsea had haphazardly taped over it. Brock came up from the schoolroom with Andrea and was quickly ushered into the family room but not before I caught a glimpse of his wide eyes as he whispered, "Police!"

The ambulance was hardly visible as it approached the stain glass window and Clara led me outside. A stretcher waited for me outside the door, I obediently crawled into it, trying to hide the shakiness that had overcome me. I clutched Pom defensively as straps were tightened around my chest, legs, and waist. I was rolled into the back of the ambulance and watched as Clara climbed in behind me and sat on the bench next to me. A blood pressure cuff was applied to my arm and began taking my vitals as we drove away from the facility I called my home.

Clara and I started to tell stories, laugh, and sign to each other to ease the anxiety we felt. I watched as the road behind us flew by and the gray skies appeared more monotone than before. The ride was bumpy, we laughed each time Clara was jostled without a seatbelt to hold her in place. The ambulance drivers talked amongst themselves in front of us, paying no attention to the happy facades we indulged in. We signed obscene and obscure things to each other, desperate to brighten the mood.

Eventually, the ambulance came to a stop in the parking bay leading to the Emergency Room. I was rolled into the Emergency Room of St. Louis Children's hospital before I was unstrapped and allowed to walk with Clara to sign in. We waited for a while, watching children in varying conditions come in to wait beside us. She scrolled through her TikTok feed, allowing me to peer over her shoulder and watch with her. Eventually, she was called into a small room to check in. She waved at me through the window as I nervously pretended to be absorbed in watching the fish swim through the large aquarium.

I was called into a curtained off room with her where they assessed my wounds. The nurse tried to be overly cautious while removing the adhesive stitches covering my side despite me assuring her that I could bear the pain. I stared at Clara, wishing she would stay closer to me. Once all thirty strips were removed from the five freshest cuts, she announced that all five of them required stitches. She generously applied lidocaine gel to the area and covered them with large clear bandages before sending us back to the waiting room.

After a while of waiting, we were led through a maze of hallways to a room with the number 30 painted in large yellow numbers above the door. Nurses sat outside each of the doors, talking to one another. I was given a bag to put my clothes and shoes in and blue paper scrubs to change into. I quickly changed and invited Clara back into the room before solemnly lying on the bed. The room was empty, everything had been removed besides the plastic bed and a chair. Even so, the room was small and nearly crowded.

I hugged Pom as tears formed in my eyes. Clara sat at the edge of the bed, instead of the chair and asked gently, "Are you ok, buddy?"

I stifled a sniffle, "I'm scared, I don't know what's going on. You said I'd be home for dinner, right?"

"I didn't know this would happen. I'm just as confused as you are," she admitted. "I'm sure you'll be home for dinner. Do you want to hear something funny?" I nodded. "I tried to tell them I was your tech at the facility, and they wrote down that I was your foster mom, so I guess I'm your foster mom today."

I giggled as a tear fell down my cheek. I wished I had a mom like Clara, someone who couldn't care less that I was trans and could indulge in a fit of laughter with me. I never laughed at my house. I was overjoyed to play into this fantasy for a day and my tears dissipated. "Can I call you mom?"

"I like mama better," she replied playfully.

"Ok, mama," I smiled. Clara couldn't love me, it was unethical, but for one day I could pretend that the familial love I felt for her was reciprocated. I could pretend that a magical fairy had taken me away from my house forever and I never had to go back, and I lived with someone who loved me as I was. It was a glorious fantasy.

As different nurses came in and out of the room, we continued to pretend that Clara was my foster mother and I slowly perked up. We giggled when they asked her questions about my home life or fostering. The fantasy kept my fears at bay and the creeping suspicion that I wouldn't be home for dinner from darkening my mind. One nurse even said we looked alike even though we couldn't have looked more different. Her hair was dyed a deep red, while mine was its natural shade of blonde, and our facial features bore no similarities besides the blue in our eyes.

At last, it was time for me to get stitches. I laid on my side and anxiously waited for the sensation of a needle penetrating my skin. I felt nothing but an indistinct tugging as Clara's eyes shifted nervously from my face to my side. *I'm tired, mama,* I signed to her as I began to relax. I heard the nurses above me counting the stitches but was unable to see anything besides Clara and the bottom half of the nurses. Clara signed something obscene to me and the nurses instructed her not to make me laugh as I giggled in response. She turned her phone to me, and I read her message to Reya explaining the situation. Reya's response, "*Jesus take the wheel.*" nearly threw me into another fit of laughter. I ended up getting thirty-one stitches, six in three of the cuts, nine on the longest gash, and four on the shortest one.

When the nurses were finished stitching me up, the large clock on the wall bore the numbers 5:20 in bright red numbers. Clara's shift was nearly over, and I begged her to stay with me. I had waited to see Kayliegh all day, but I had been told that she was staying with Brock, and Wanda, a tech I had never met before, was coming to stay with me instead. My pleas were ignored and soon Wanda had replaced Clara's spot in the chair beside my bed. The lidocaine was slowly wearing off and my side was burning intensely.

Wanda made me eat dinner as I hadn't eaten since breakfast, hospital chicken nuggets and tater tots. She showed me her photography and let me draw in her sketchbook as we waited to leave. I was even able to call Kayleigh on her phone and talk to her briefly. I attempted to call Bronwyn as well, but she didn't pick up. Wanda was sweet, but I really wanted to go home and see Kayleigh. The hours passed slowly and painfully as I listened to the cries and groans of children in the other rooms.

Finally, a screen on a stand was rolled into my room and I was able to talk to the psychiatrist who would decide whether I was able to leave. I put on a happy face and answered all the questions correctly. Even so, they decided to admit me. My heart broke when the nurse came in and said, "You're not going home today." I could feel tears well up in my eyes but held it together until Wanda left an hour later. I didn't want to concern her because I knew that would push her to stay longer and I wanted to fall apart alone.

As soon as she left, I began to cry. At first, I tried to be quiet but as I stared at the clock every minute passing by made it more clear that I really wasn't leaving. I began to cry louder, it was an uncontainable sob. After two hours of crying, a nurse peeked into the room and asked, "What's wrong?"

"I'm sad," I choked out.

"You're sad? Well keep your head up, little guy," he mumbled before walking away.

I wasn't consoled and continued to cry myself to sleep, hugging Pom.

The next morning, I woke up around eleven and began to cry again immediately. I was alone in the room now, completely and utterly alone. I had no way to talk to my friends, or to Clara, Raven, or Kayliegh. A nurse walked in to me crying and tried again to console me, it still didn't work. I requested to shower and brush my teeth, all I wanted to do was feel warm water wash over me and to feel clean. All I could control in that moment was whether or not I was clean; I pleaded to shower for the next hour.

The nurses told me I wasn't allowed to brush my teeth unless I ate. As I was escorted to the shower room by a rough security guard, I begged for a toothbrush. She laughed and told me I could brush my teeth but only with a baby toothbrush. I had to negotiate for soap and shampoo as well as they were worried I would consume it to make myself ill. Eventually, I was handed the proper toiletries and a fresh pair of paper scrubs to change into and allowed into the shower room while the security guard stood outside the door.

I turned on the water and watched it sputter out from the rusty showerhead as I got undressed and threw away the old paper scrubs. I allowed the warm water to cleanse my body as I quickly washed myself. I turned off the water and used the hand towel they had provided me to dry myself off before changing into the fresh scrubs. I brushed my teeth with the tiny toothbrush, staring at myself in the mirror forlornly. As I trudged back to my room following the security guard, I tried to tune out the yelling and screaming filling the hallway she led me to. I immediately returned to my bed and fell back asleep to pass the time.

"Get up, bud. You're leaving," a nurse spat at me.

"Really?" I nearly squealed, sitting upright.

"Yep. Here's your shirt. The place you're going doesn't allow strings so you'll have to keep wearing the scrub pants."

My expression darkened, "Where am I going?"

"A place called MidPoint. We have a driver here to take you so hurry up and change. It's cold outside, do you want a blanket?" she asked.

"No," I responded much less enthusiastically. I didn't want to go to MidPoint, I wanted to go back to Pomegranate. I changed and followed the burly man outside my door outside to the ambulance bay where a black car sat. I got in the backseat and tried not to cry.

"MidPoint isn't really that bad," the driver said. "I drive kids all over the state to different places and they all say it's one of the best places to be. They have a gym, and books, and crafts, and lots of recreational time. You'll only be there for a few days, if that's the worst thing in your life, you have a pretty good life."

I tried to be agreeable as he rambled about the worst situations kids had been in to make me feel better. He nearly convinced me to feel ok about the situation, it was only for a few days, right? It felt strange to be in a car again, I hadn't been in a car in nearly a month. I watched the other cars rush past us, hoping none of the people driving them were having as awful of a day as me. The sky was a deceivingly cheery shade of blue, but the clouds were hiding in fear of what was to come.

Chapter Eleven: Boy, Interrupted

"But I know what it's like to want to die. How it hurts to smile. How you try to fit in but you can't. You hurt yourself on the outside to try to kill the thing on the inside."

-Susanna Kaysen

We ended up at a large brick building where we had to wait for the receptionist to unlock the doors from the inside of the building before entering. There were rows of armchairs in the lobby and a large desk where the driver told the receptionist who I was. I looked around nervously as she took the plastic bag of clothes I held and locked them up. I kept my teddy bear safe in my arms as the driver left and I was directed through a maze of hallways.

I was taken into a room to wait for my evaluation. It was beige, with lines and words scratched into the walls. I sat in a large beige plastic chair opposite of another, much smaller desk. I sat with my knees up to my chest, taking up the least space possible. If I could have disappeared from that plastic chair, I would've. But I couldn't, so I sat and waited. I could hear a woman talking through the walls, asking if she could keep her cigarettes.

Finally, a frail older woman came in with a clipboard and evaluated me. I was slightly more honest with her than I was with the hospital psychiatrist since I had already been admitted, but my answers still aired on the side of caution. After the evaluation, I was strip searched and given new scrubs as my shirt was taken once again. After a thorough search and the confiscation of my remaining clothes and my teddy bear, I was led to the adolescent unit.

The adolescent unit was housed in a narrow hallway and had many doors. I was placed in a small blue chair across from the nurses' desk where they gave me a new hospital bracelet, took my vitals, and gave me a sample cup to urinate in. I was given a folder, a composition notebook, and a dull pencil to write with and instructed to join the other kids in the dayroom. The dayroom was a large room with many tables and more of the beige plastic chairs. They were too heavy to move

106

around, supposedly filled with sand. The time was around 7:00 p.m. and the kids were watching TV absentmindedly.

I immediately started writing a letter to Bronwyn in the notebook, scribbling furiously:

3/9/23

Dear Bronwyn,

I'm in a different place now for a little while. Let me fill you in.

I continued to scribble out the events of the day until a boy I had seen in the emergency room peered over my shoulder and began reading the letter out loud. I was astounded by his lack of boundaries and stared at him incredulously.

"Oh, so you're here for..." he made a slicing motion on his arm. "That sucks, I hope you get out soon. I'm Pierce and I'm here because I held a gun to my head."

With that abrupt introduction, he walked away. I sat there for a second, stunned, before finishing my letter:

I'm just going to be on my best behavior so I can leave and go back to Pomegranate.

I love and miss you very much.

<3333,

Faber Elliott

At 9:00 in the evening, I was rushed into my room for bed. The room was small, with a door to the bathroom next to the door leading to the room, a sink behind the door, two beds behind the sink, a large, barred window across from the door, and a single wooden shelf mounted to the wall. The beds were plastic mattresses encased in a wooden block that was screwed into the floor. I laid in the bed closest to the door and attempted to sleep. It was impossible, the room was freezing cold, and I could hear my rhythmic heartbeat in my head when I pressed my ear against the pillow.

I laid awake, not even closing my eyes for a while. Every half hour, a nurse would peek their head in the doorway, allowing light to spill in from the hallway. After a while, a nurse came into the room and walked towards the bed. I squeezed my eyes closed, feigning sleep as she drew closer. A loud thud forced my eyes to open again.

The nurse's eyes widened as she stared at me, "I'm so sorry, I didn't mean to wake you!"

"It's ok, I wasn't really sleeping." I admitted sheepishly. The nurse's name tag read "Lacey," her brown hair was put in a braid that grazed her back, her gentle features put me at ease.

"Can I turn the light on?" she asked, still holding the pillow that had thudded against the other bed. I told her she could, and she proceeded to wipe down the other plastic mattress and make the bed. "You're getting a roommate, his name is Axel. Are you too anxious to sleep?"

"Yeah, I'm pretty anxious," I replied.

"What are you in for? Psych or Substances?"

"Psych, I had to get stitches for self harm and they sent me here." I explained.

She gently passed on a few cliché phrases about the value of life and how things were bound to get better as I watched her finish making the bed. She left briefly and returned with my new roommate. His hair was carelessly shaved and he was tall. He wore the same light blue scrubs as me. Lacey gave him a quick room tour before leaving us alone.

Axel started telling me his story as I did my best to seem interested. I craved sleep, the numb feeling, the unconscious passing of time. Eventually, I told him I was going to sleep and returned to lying awake listening to my heartbeat and shivering under the knitted white blanket. I tried desperately to find a comfortable position but redundantly failed. Soon sleep overtook me and I was blissfully unaware of my current situation.

"Get up! Time for vitals!" a voice boomed from the doorway.

I rolled out of bed slowly and peeked out of the open doorway, watching children file out of their rooms with frizzy hair and weary expressions. I followed them to line up behind a chair sitting in the middle of the hallway. When it was my turn, I sat in the chair as they took my blood pressure and temperature before dismissing me. On top of a small rolling cabinet, I searched for the Styrofoam cup with my name on it. I found it quickly, it had a toothbrush, comb, toothpaste, and roll on deodorant inside.

I took it back to my room and looked at my messy hair in the mirror. We were only allowed to shower in the evening, so I pushed down the button on the sink and forced my head under the faucet to allow the water to trickle through my hair. I grabbed a paper towel from the neat stack on the edge of the sink to dry it slightly before combing it and fluffing it up a bit. I brushed my teeth as Axel finally got out of bed.

I left the room to return my cup and join the children in the dayroom for breakfast. I sat across from a bigger person with curly black hair. They ate ferociously as I sat without even touching my tray. Other kids indulged in the toast, sausages, and eggs provided to them, but I couldn't have been less hungry. I sipped on a small plastic cup of apple juice, figuring it would keep my blood sugar up so I wouldn't feel ill from refusing to eat. I dumped the food into the trashcan and returned the tray to the food cart before finding my notebook and starting a new letter to Bronwyn.

Later in the day, some kids were able to leave the dayroom to go to the gym. Everyone who had been at MidPoint for less than a day was still on UR, or Unit Restriction, and were forced to stay in the dayroom. I recognized a few kids from the rooms near me at the hospital and we began to share our stories. A girl named Livi was from the room across from me and had been sent to MidPoint after a nurse noticed the scars on her arms. She told me I was the first indicator to her that she was in the psychiatric section of the hospital, or rather my scar filled arms were.

As it was my first day, I also met with the psychiatrist. She had a thick Indian accent and was difficult to understand. She ate throughout our meeting, speaking with mouthfuls of food that made it even more difficult to comprehend what she was saying.

"Are you trans because something bad happened?" she asked while chewing on popcorn.

"No, I'm just more comfortable living as a boy," I responded, attempting not to roll my eyes at the ignorant comment.

"Have you ever been to a mental hospital before?"

"No, this is my first time in a facility like this," I mumbled.

"Really?" she said as her eyes assessed my arms condescendingly. "With all those scars nobody *ever* thought to take you to a mental hospital?" she spat.

I shifted uncomfortably, wishing I could detach my arms from my body and hide them away. "No."

"Impressive!" she snarled. "Well, it's clear to me that you need heavy medications."

She began listing medications she was prescribing me as she scribbled them down. Lithium, Ativan, an antipsychotic, the list was endless. I was also put on a two hour bathroom restriction as she didn't believe that my eating disorder didn't entail purging. This meant that I wasn't allowed to use the restroom for two hours after meals were served. When she finished, she handed me a phone and asked me to call my mom to consent to the medications. She watched me dial the number before leaving the room to grab her next patient.

110

My mom picked up as tears were forming in my eyes. I urgently whispered, "Mom, this is horrible, they're going to overmedicate me. Please don't consent to these medications, it's Ativan and really heavy stuff. And please don't visit, it's so awful here."

By the last sentence, the psychiatrist had returned and grabbed the phone from me. "No more time for talking, she has to go now. Please visit even if she asks you not to. You can call the front desk to consent to the medications, have a nice day!"

And with that, I was taken out of the room and put back into the dayroom where I wrote to Bronwyn about my awful experience.

3/10/23

Dear Bronwyn,

I'm not sure if you've noticed I'm gone yet or if you'll notice at all, but I miss talking to you. I saw your email right before I got in the ambulance, but I didn't have time to respond. You look so beautiful in your prom dress, and I can't wait to tell you that.

A bunch of people who came on the same day as me have already had breakdowns. I haven't yet, I'm on my best behavior, I need to leave. I'm waiting for Pomegranate to call, they said they would be in contact with me every day. Maybe if Kayleigh is working, I can say hi to her.

They talked to us about the restraint chair today. It seems pretty traumatic, but they said it's a last resort. Two adults have already had a code green called on them today. Code green means you're uncontrollable and that's when they bring in the restraint chair. It's a big metal chair with straps for your arms, legs, and chests. There's one around every corner here to remind you to behave.

Our unit is completely full right now, there's a lot of kids here. I've made some friends but I'm not getting too close to anyone because I can't handle being separated from another person I love in such a short amount of time.

I love and miss you a ton.

<3333,

Faber Elliott

My roommate, Axel became very dependent on me immediately. They had Dissociative Identity Disorder and often needed to be reminded where they were and what they were doing. I had to ask the nurses for food, drinks, and band aids for them when they picked at their scabs. The nurses noticed this clinginess and threatened to separate us but after Axel became visibly upset, they let the idea go. I secretly wished to be separated from them, caring for them had quickly become tiring.

The next morning, I awoke covered in blood, I had started my period. I asked the nurse for a tampon and new scrubs and went to the only unlocked bathroom to clean myself up. The tampons had cardboard applicators and were difficult to use, which only added to my frustration. This was the worst place in the world to be on your period. I was hardly even allowed to go to the restroom due to my bathroom restriction. I was able to clean myself up and discreetly throw away the soiled scrubs before walking out into the adjacent room that was identical to my own.

I stood in the doorway to line up for vitals and felt a sharp pain in my foot. I looked down to see that Livi had fallen on me, blocking the doorway. I backed up into the room as she began to violently tremble and seize. A general pandemonium ensued as the other kids were ushered into the dayroom and I stood watching the nurses crowd Livi as a code blue was announced over the loudspeakers. She continued to seize as a nurse came running down the hallway with a metal cart full of medical devices. Eventually, they were able to stabilize her and the line for vitals formed once again in the hallway.

After I had finished vitals, I sat in the dayroom and began working on the paperwork I needed to move up to Level One in the level system. The level system was a way for patients to earn privileges through good behavior and paperwork detailing their goals, shortcomings, story, and knowledge of the medications they were prescribed. Truthfully, I didn't care what level I was on, what I cared about were the privileges that came with moving up in the system. People on Level One earned their clothes back. I couldn't wait to change out of the thin paper scrubs.

As I scribbled through my paperwork, the dayroom filled and kids began eating their breakfasts. I gave mine to the kid across from me as there were no staff present to watch us eat. A few moments later, one of the kids began to yell, "Staff! Staff!" I looked over, Livi had passed out again in front of her tray.

I went over to her table and joined the chant of "Staff! Staff!" that had engulfed the room. We watched helplessly as she began to seize and nobody came to monitor her. After a few minutes, a staff member finally walked into the room and rushed out quickly to call a code blue.

We were instructed to sit in the doorways of our rooms in front of the locked doors. Two kids to each doorway, all wearing blue paper scrubs and a solemn look. It was a scene straight out of a movie, a movie you would never want to live through but watched for your own curiosity and entertainment. We sat, whispering to each other as the nurse came running through the hall with the metal cart once more. I craned my neck, attempting to see what was going on in the dayroom, but was unable to see anything. Finally, a stretcher was rolled through the hallway to carry Livi away and we were led back to the dayroom as if nothing ever happened.

I finished my paperwork and turned it in to the nurses, anxious to receive my clothes in return. I frequently peered at the whiteboard displaying our levels and watched as everybody's levels changed except mine. I had to ask the nurses several times to review my paperwork before they finally erased "Entry" from my level indicator and replaced it with a "1." Still, no clothes came, and I was promised they would be given to me the next day.

I met with the psychiatrist again, who irritably informed me that my parents had not consented to any of the medications she had prescribed me. I hid the smile of relief pulling at my cheeks as she crunched through a handful of chips. Our meeting was short as there was nothing she could do for me any longer. She asked me to grab Axel for her as she continued to shove chips into her mouth.

I walked to the dayroom to find Axel with his hands propping up his head. I called his name, gently at first, growing into a urgent plea. He didn't move, he appeared to be frozen in time and his eyes had glazed over. I moved closer to him until I was gently nudging his arm with no response. His arms collapsed suddenly, driving his head into the table. I ran back to the psychiatrist's office to alert her.

"I think Axel's having a seizure!" I informed her.

She stared at me blankly before peering into the dayroom and returning to flipping through papers. I ran to check on Axel, who was now shaking uncontrollably. The other kids had curled up or sat back in their chairs, clearly distressed. I ran to tell the nurses, they also stared at me blankly and made no move to help. I jogged back to the dayroom and crouched down beside Axel, watching him twitch and tremble. I waited for a staff member to come help him, I was met with the silence of a dozen frightened children.

Finally, a nurse walked into the dayroom and called a code blue. We were instructed to sit in our doorways again. We hissed to each other about the clear neglect the staff had shown but sat obediently in front of our locked doors. The metal cart was brought down the hallway once again as the hallway filled with muffled yells for Axel to wake up.

"It's probably the lithium," a blonde girl named Samantha whispered from the end of the hallway. "We're all on it."

"All of you?" I asked. Heads nodded in response.

"They hand it out like Halloween candy around here," a brunette girl responded. Her name was Fallon, we hadn't acknowledged each other yet, but she was undoubtably the most stunning person in the facility. I wanted to become friends with her, maybe more than friends, but I had hardly even heard her voice until now. "I think she only knows a few medications and prescribes the same ones to everybody. Let me guess, she prescribed you Lithium, Ativan, and Latuda?"

"And a few more," I admitted. "I told my parents not to consent, so I don't have to take them."

"Lucky!" Samantha whispered. "My head is always fuzzy and I can't focus on anything, it's terrible."

Axel walked out of the dayroom shakily and all eyes turned toward him as he sat down next to me. We went quiet as the nurse unlocked our rooms for room time. Room time was a one-hour period of the day where we were forced to sit in our empty rooms with nothing to do while the staff switched out. I always attempted to nap, but it was impossible with Axel constantly switching into a confused fluster demanding to know where they were. I went into our room and laid on my bed, clinging to the thin sheets as I forced my eyes to close.

I had nearly fallen asleep when Axel mumbled, "Faber, I feel fuzzy."

"Fuzzy?" I groaned. "What do you mean fuzzy?"

"Like I'm about to have a seizure," he explained.

Are you serious? Another one? That's four in one day. I sat up, "Do you want me to go get someone?"

"No, they're mean. Just sit here and watch me, ok?"

"Ok, but if you have a seizure, I'm going to go get someone."

I sat and watched him as he slowly slipped away from being in control of his body and eventually fell into a pile on his bed. His head dangled dangerously close to the wooden frame of the bed so I got up and started to readjust him. With a lot of effort, I pulled his legs onto the bed and grabbed his spiky shaved head to gently rest it on his pillow. My poor strength left his body slightly curved, but in a safe position.

I grabbed a nurse, this time no code blue was called. I sat in the doorway, talking to the other kids as she handled Axel. I watched as a new admittance entered the ward, a tall, strong, tan boy with jet black hair. He was incredibly handsome despite the ill-fitting blue scrubs, and I watched his admittance with interest while the girls started whispering to each other. Room time always felt unbearably long, I compulsively checked the clock at the end of the hallway every few minutes.

When room time finally ended, I was exhausted but a plan had formed in my head. Today was visiting day and I was sure my parents would come. I started a new letter detailing the horrors of this place, the neglect, having to help Axel with everything, the psychiatrist prescribing the same meds to everyone, having to earn our clothes. When I wrote it all down, it seemed extremely dramatic, so I passed it around the room for people to proofread it. Everyone agreed that it was entirely truthful and not hyperbolized, so I folded it up and hid it in my sock to ensure the staff wouldn't find it or take it away.

"I'll buy you a Diet Coke if you're able to give the letter to your parents today," Fallon offered.

"Really?" I had been staring at the Diet Coke in the cafeteria vending machine every dinner period when we were allowed to visit the cafeteria. We weren't allowed any diet sodas at Pomegranate, and they looked so cold and delicious.

"Really. I hope they can get you out of here," she replied.

We went down to the warm cafeteria, and I sipped on an orange juice as everyone anxiously guessed who would come to visit them. I still couldn't force myself to eat as I explained how I was hoping someone from Pomegranate would visit me. I told them about Clara, Raven, and Kayliegh and how wonderful they were. We went back up to our unit and a few people showered to prepare for their visits, but I decided to wait until afterwards.

The cafeteria was also the place visits were hosted and those of us with visitors were led back there at 7:00 p.m. sharp. My brother and mom sat at a table. I crossed my arms shamefully, my brother had never seen my scars before. I slipped the note to my mother and a few seconds later Fallon placed a Diet Coke in front of me which I happily sipped on. I pleaded with my mom to call the front desk and ask them to discharge me and she told me they were doing what they could. My brother informed me that they no longer believed my story about the pencil but couldn't find another source of the injuries and that's why I hadn't been discharged yet.

The meeting ended before I had finished my Diet Coke, so I threw the remainder of it in the garbage and followed Samantha and Fallon back to the unit. I showered and prepared for bed before finishing my daily letter to Bronwyn and watching TV until it was time to go to our rooms.

The next morning, as I lined up for vitals, I could hear the nurse murmuring to someone on the phone. "Our typical stay length is five to seven days, she really hasn't been here long enough."

I wondered if someone from my facility was trying to get me discharged and eagerly tried to make out more of the conversation. I was interrupted by Pierce bragging that his parents had called to have him discharged and he was going home today. If the phone call was about me, they were clearly lying because Pierce had gotten here on the same day as I had. I turned my attention back to the phone call before turning my head to follow a retching sound coming from the direction of my room. Axel appeared and informed the nurse that he had thrown up to which they responded that he could go back to sleep. *Thank god, I don't have to take care of them today.*

Before I could even grab the small Styrofoam cup housing my toiletries, a nurse instructed me to follow her. I was taken into a small, cluttered room to have my blood drawn. I had already gotten my blood drawn upon my admission, but they claimed to have lost the sample of my blood. I happily allowed them to draw more, relishing the sharp sting of the needle. They allowed me to pick a few pieces of candy, which I dealt out to my friends.

My clothes had finally appeared in a brown bag in my room, and I put the pajama pants and t-shirt on gratefully before returning to the dayroom to fill out my daily goals sheet. W (my wish): To be discharged. O (best outcome): I will leave and be so happy. O (my obstacle): I haven't been here long enough. P (my plan): When I want to leave, I will turn off my feelings until I don't care anymore. I had taken a bit of a brutally honest approach to the worksheet, but I no longer cared about the consequences.

During room time, Axel had another seizure. A nurse came to check on him, but decided to leave me alone to watch over him. His shaking hands began to hit his face and he started to slip off of the bed as he wheezed for breath. I went over to his bed and held his hands away from his face and kept him from falling off the bed as tears formed in my eyes. It was my job to keep him safe, there was nobody to help.

I saw Fallon walk past my doorway and called out to her for help. She ran to grab a nurse and I heard the metal cart rolling down the hallway once again. The nurse smacked me away from Axel, we weren't allowed to touch and it was her way of reprimanding me. I got back into my own bed and pulled the covers over my head. They had finally given me my teddy bear back and I held onto him as they shuffled around the room. Eventually, the seizure ended, and room time was over.

I called my parents during the ten minute phone times and wrote to Bronwyn about the news they gave me.

My facility DID try to get me out! They told them they don't do discharges on the weekends which is such a lie! Three people got discharged this weekend but they're lying to keep me longer. I'll definitely get out this week though, hopefully tomorrow or Tuesday. I'm going to have a piece of cake (today's snack) to celebrate. I haven't eaten since I got here, I've definitely relapsed in my eating disorder, but this is an occasion for some cake!

I ate my cake and crawled into bed. Axel and I had finally been separated due to his overdependence on me and I slept blissfully in the silence. I hoped to go home the following day, home being Pomegranate. The hope kept me warm even in the bitter cold of my room. I had a dream about reuniting with Jolene, Devyn, and Callie. It was a happy reunification, although I wasn't sure Jolene and Devyn cared about me anymore in the waking world.

The next day, a new staff member was in charge. He spoke with a militant voice and called me "little lady," which I hated immensely. He asked us immediately upon waking up to read the thirteen page long rulebook. Fallon was assigned to read, but it was slow and painful.

"Can I read instead?" I asked with a fake politeness. He nodded and I began where Fallon left off, reading faster than a professional rapper. "The following items are not permitted on the unit: Alcohol, drugs, paraphernalia, tobacco products, weapons, matches, lighters, belts, books or magazines promoting drugs, alcohol, sex, or violence, CD's, tapes, audio, or video, walk-man radio/tapes..." There was half a page of contraband items separated only by spaces and the kids began to giggle as I read it as quickly as the speech at the end of a radio advertisement.

I sped through the following eight pages of rules until the end of the final page when the man, Mr. Jeff, said, "Nice job, little lady."

The giggling in the room ceased and faces turned alert as people watched for my reaction. I gave no indication that it bothered me, I could tell Mr. Jeff would not handle my feelings with compassion. I nodded and Mr. Jeff continued to berate us about the rules as we sat together in the melancholy knowledge that this man was the worst staff member we'd faced yet. He yelled at us for nearly an hour before instructing us to write down steps we would take to behave that day.

He left the room to discuss something with the nurses and around twenty minutes later, Axel cried out, "Faber!"

I got to him just in time to break his fall before he started seizing again.

"Don't touch her!" Mr. Jeff yelled from the hallway. I scrambled backwards and let him slump against the wall. Mr. Jeff grabbed a wheelchair, lifted Axel into it and started heading into the hallway.

"Support his head!" several people shouted at him. As he reached the doorway, Axel's unsupported head fell forward, leading the rest of his body towards the floor before Mr. Jeff caught him. This was the final straw after an already long day of being beaten down and several people began to cry.

"Get in your rooms, all of you!" Mr. Jeff yelled as a nurse started unlocking the doors. "We're shutting down the whole unit, you brats!" Everyone shuffled to their doorways, most people wiping away their tears simultaneously. "No standing in the doorways! Lay on your beds until I say you can leave! I don't want to see a single face out here!"

I stole a look at myself in the mirror before heading to my bed. My eyes were wide and unblinking with dilated pupils, the dark circles under them were more pronounced than ever. Several people had informed me that my appearance was tragic, but I wasn't prepared to see a face that appeared to have just returned from Hell. I sat in my bed alone listening to muffled sniffing coming from other rooms. I stared at the beige wall holding my teddy bear for what felt like an eternity.

Three hours later, we were let out of our rooms. I walked into the hallway and nearly screamed; my name was on the discharge board! I was finally going to leave! Fallon's name had also been written on the board and we looked at each other, grinning from ear to ear. She was scheduled to leave only fifteen minutes before me the following day. I sat next to her in the dayroom until a nurse came to grab me.

"Have you been drinking anything?" she asked.

I hadn't been. Due to my bathroom restriction, I had stopped drinking almost entirely out of the fear of not being allowed to go to the restroom when I needed to. "A little," I lied.

"Your calcium is through the roof, you're extremely dehydrated. Your kidneys are going to dry up," she explained. I suppose they should have thought about that before restricting my bathroom use.

I assured her I would drink more with no intention of following through with the promise. I was leaving the next day, one more day of dehydration couldn't cause much harm. I was told that Fallon would be my roommate during our last night at the facility. I was elated, Fallon was the best roommate I could possibly ask for. She was calm and levelheaded, a rare trait to possess in a place like this. When it came time to go to our rooms for the night, Fallon and I talked for hours about our lives and our friends before finally falling asleep.

The next morning, we woke up smiling. We requested to shower in the morning instead of attending gym so we could be clean and well-groomed upon our discharge. The staff agreed and I nearly giggled as the hot water fell over me. I combed my hair carefully and got dressed before meeting Fallon in the dayroom where we laughed joyously and reveled in the idea of leaving. We were told to write a paragraph about someone we missed while we waited when we became too loud and obnoxious for the staff to handle.

3/14/23

I miss my best friend Bronwyn dearly. I haven't seen her since my hospitalization in January since I live three hours away and haven't been home since then. I have gotten to talk to her on the phone twice since then and when I had my cell phone, she sent me pictures everyday telling me how much she loves and misses me. I hope she wasn't too worried when I stopped responding to her emails when I came here. I write her letters everyday telling her how much I love and miss her.

Fallon was called to leave, and I began to swing my legs in anticipation. I hoped Clara would pick me up or that I would at least get to see her at the facility when I got back. It was Tuesday, my favorite day, Reya, Clara, Kayleigh, KV, and Raven should all be there. *All my favorite people should be there!* It was almost too good to be true. As time passed, I began to worry that it *was* too good to be true. The clock had passed 10:30 and still I sat waiting.

Finally, a nurse called, "Time to go!"

Chapter Twelve: Burst Bubble

"Let the guilty bury the innocent, and let no one change the evidence."

-Ian McEwan

I walked through the hallways of the building I was desperate to escape clutching my bag of possessions. An escort led me to the lobby, and I peered around for a second before finding Raven sitting in an armchair.

"Raven!" I exclaimed, feeling the flush of a smile fill my cheeks. I ran to her, I would have hugged her if we were allowed to, but instead I stood in front of her eagerly.

"Here's the rest of your stuff," the escort stated blandly, pointing to a large plastic tote. I had more stuff? Many of the clothing items were things I had never worn or seen before, but the escort insisted it was mine, so I shoved it all into my paper bag and headed for the automatic doors.

I skipped through the parking lot before allowing Raven to catch up to lead me to where she had parked. "Raven, it was so awful there!" I groaned. "I can't wait to get back to Pomegranate. Nobody there cared about us, it was unbearably horrible."

I told her a few of the details on the ride home but left long silences to enjoy the music playing on the radio. I hadn't heard music since I'd been at Pomegranate. The sweet harmonies flooded my ears and quieted my mind. When we pulled into the driveway of Pomegranate, I hopped out of the van and rushed inside, eager to close the door behind me and solidify that I was home. Brock sat playing computer games and didn't even acknowledge my entrance. Clara wasn't there as she was likely on her break and Reya sat at the small round corner table watching Brock.

"Welcome back, Fabes!" Reya announced.

"Thank you!" I squealed as I ran to my spot on the couch, the spot Taylor had given me when she left. I didn't want to share my experiences in front of Brock so I sat quietly, staring at the door to ensure it wouldn't open again. The TV wasn't playing so we sat in an awkward silence, but this felt like a situation where one should enable the "If you don't have anything good to say, don't say anything at all," policy.

I was called back by the nurse to have a skin check and my clothes checked to ensure I didn't bring anything dangerous back from MidPoint. I had to retake the long survey I had to take when I had first gotten to Pomegranate to measure the severity of my eating disorder, depression, and anxiety. They informed me that there were no significant changes in my results, which was a bit discouraging. It made sense, I hadn't eaten in days and the results reflected the slip.

Finally, Clara walked in and it was time to sit down for lunch. Brock had already eaten, so I was alone at the table with Raven and Clara. Now that I was in a safe environment to eat, I happily indulged. Lunch was a ham and cheese sandwich on a croissant served with chips on the side. I flapped my hands and bounced around joyfully as I ate and listened to the music Clara was playing on a Bluetooth speaker.

"I'm so hungry," I explained. "I couldn't get myself to eat the whole time I was there. It was so awful." Raven and Clara sat silently, eating along with me. I was so glad to be back, but I knew I wasn't better.

Days passed in the same fashion they had before. I self-harmed with the blade everyone knew existed, but couldn't find, got caught, made up a story about what I used, and continued to stumble through my day. I told Cendall about my awful stay at MidPoint and she was sympathetic. I was still on safety observations, sleeping in a cot in the hallway rather than in a bed. The days were mundane, but that was much preferred over the chaos of Midpoint.

After three days of being back and two incidents of self-harm, Caprese, the site manager, called me back to her office with Cendall. I sat down as she closed the door and said, "Faber, we're not stupid, we know you have something. Nursing said it's not possible to cause that kind of damage with a pencil"

"I threw it away already," I lied. I was completely cornered but determined to lie my way out of it.

"Faber, if you don't hand it over, we can't keep you here. You'll have to go back to MidPoint or Hawkins which is even worse. So, are you going to hand it over?" Cendall urged.

"I don't want to," I admitted, frozen in fear of their threat. I couldn't go back, there was no lying my way out of things this time.

"I know you don't want to, but would you rather do that or go to another ward? If you go to a ward, you won't be coming back this time," Caprese doubled down.

I wouldn't get to graduate from the program or spend any more time with Kayleigh, Clara, Raven, or Reya. "Fine, I'll give it to you."

"We tried to trust you, Faber. We tried to let you do this on your own terms but it's far too severe to keep waiting. We have a responsibility to keep you safe and this is the only way."   My cheeks flushed with shame and I kept my eyes on the ground as I led Cendall to my bathroom, reached for the back of the toilet, and carefully folded the deodorant label over the sharp edge of the blade before handing it to Cendell. She thanked me and asked me how I got it into the facility in the first place. I explained to her how I had put it inside my floss container, wrapped in a piece of toilet paper to prevent it from rattling around inside of it. I was led back to the milieu as the staff held a meeting to discuss this new information.

It was gone, the only thing that kept me sane. I immediately began tearing skin off of my fingers until they stung and bled. I used to pick my skin frequently, but the behavior had disappeared for the most part until then. I was given Band-Aids and laid down for a nap to forget the events of the day. I played music softly in one earbud through my iPod Nano 3rd Generation, listening to the underlying chords rather than the lyrics and slowly drifted to sleep.

When I woke up, Brock had turned on a World War II documentary and was being scolded for swaying side to side while watching it. Any unnecessary movements were strongly discouraged at Pomegranate as they had the potential to burn calories. Ideally, you were meant to sit or lie down unless you had to walk to a new destination to sit down. Even standing for more than a few seconds was prohibited. Of course, as soon as I woke up, he began to inquire about where I had been and what it was like. He claimed his uncle worked in a psychiatric hospital and told horror stories. I didn't desire to share my own. It was over now, reliving it didn't appeal to me.

Brock transitioned to watching Miley Cyrus' Wrecking Ball music video on the computer and when I shot him a look he whispered, "Snitches get stitches."

Without thinking, I replied, "I already got some." His eyes widened as he put the pieces together and I nearly ran my head into my palm for telling him what had happened.

We went into the kitchen to portion snack and Brock nicknamed me "Patrick Swayze" after finding out I had gotten stitches. I didn't understand the reference, but I had little appreciation for being summed up to the boy who got stitches. I didn't feel like much of a person at all anymore, I was quickly losing myself. I often thought about the empty seats at school that I once filled and wondered if my classmates ever looked at them and thought about me. I wondered if my name still floated around the hallways, if anyone cared how I was doing at all.

I sat down for snack, picking at the crackers on my plate robotically. "You know," Brock began. "You really need to just love your parents. That's what you're supposed to do."

"It's more complicated than that, Brock. It's not that I don't love them, it's just complicated right now," I shot back with a sigh.

"You need parents like mine," he retorted. "Actually, they would kick you out for being trans."

"Brock!" Clara intervened. "Why would you say that?"

"My parents threatened that too," I told him quietly. I knew Brock had no idea what he was saying, I remember when I was sheltered like him. I didn't blame him and I wasn't mad, I was hurt by the reminder that I was not a desirable son.

"You can do what you want with your body," he continued. "I just don't agree with your gender."

"Don't you think I act just as much like a boy as you do?" I asked him.

"Well yeah, you're a lot like my little brother. But you weren't born that way, it's still wrong," he concluded.

"I think by the time you leave, you'll change your mind. You don't have to agree with me, you just have to be respectful. So far, you've done a decent job at it," I encouraged.

"Did I offend you?" he asked suddenly. He was starting to mature, little by little. When I had first arrived, he would have offended anyone without thinking twice or apologizing. He was working on empathy with his therapist and this simple question showed progress.

"Yes," I responded gently. "I don't think you meant to though, so I forgive you. Just be a little more careful next time."

I couldn't be mad at Brock even when he said the most outrageous things. I saw my younger self in him, the little girl who read the Bible to escape from her "sins," the girl who sat in a pew praying to be washed clean. Children's opinions are a direct reflection of the views of their caretakers. Growing up in a more conservative household myself, I likely would have regurgitated similar quips had I been in this situation at his age. Nothing he could possibly say would diminish the innocence he held in my mind.

I silently communicated to Clara that it was alright, and she didn't need to have a discussion with him before walking to put my plate and cup on the counter by the sink. I claimed the computer before Brock was able to sit down at the desk and pull up a game. I had periodically been checking Michael's case, waiting for the sentencing to be made public. I decided to do this once more and looked up my county's court records. In the search field, I typed "Michael D. Schnieder," and clicked on the result that popped up with his correct age, 34 years old.

I went into his records, found his current charges and pulled up all the information. It took me a second to process what I saw, he had been found guilty on all counts and the sentencing was now public information. I quickly did some mental math to add up the sentence lengths of his multitude of charges. He had taken a plea deal to reduce the 135 counts of child pornography to only six counts. Even still, his sentence added up to 88 years. *Eighty-eight years*. He was never leaving jail; he would never be free.

I almost screamed in a mixture of terror and shock. I couldn't wrap my head around the information. He was a despicable person, eighty-eight years was not a light sentence, and he had hugged me. He was terrible and he had touched me with his slimy hands. I had sang to him, sharing my most valuable possession. He had felt my heartbeat and my breathing, he had felt the life inside of me. And yet, he was horrible and sick. I was going to run away to his house, I was going to fall into his trap. It couldn't be true. I knew all along that it was, but now it couldn't be. I was dirty. His voice had touched my ears, the fingerprints that were now evidence of his criminal identity had once touched me. It was wretched, it was disgusting.

It was often said that at Pomegranate, we lived in a bubble. We had little access to the internet, news, or live TV. We were sheltered from the outside world in every way possible. We only ever had the opportunity to leave the lavish house twice a week at the most. My bubble had burst, and it had been done by my own hands. I read articles on Michael, finding out more grotesque details of what he had done than I had even imagined. He was truly evil in its purest form.

I closed the tab and pretended nothing was wrong, pulling out my iPod and listening to music while playing the built in Solitaire game. It was hard to focus, harder still to maintain an unphased expression. I looked out of the window and a scene flashed in front of me. In it, I stood on the three-story high balcony, turned to face Clara and bid her goodbye, and jumped. My body contorted on the pavement, my ribs heaved and shuttered with each partial breath before I stopped breathing. I would never have to feel anything again. A few moments of intense suffering for the reward of eternal peace. It seemed like a fair trade.

I played the scene repeatedly, beginning to obsess over it. I saw the terrified expression on the faces watching me, the way they ran towards me, reaching out to stop me. I saw my hair whip in the wind during my descent. I saw the sky above me, the clouds quickly becoming further away, the sun hurting my eyes. I heard the sound of my body smashing into the pavement, shattering into pieces upon impact. I saw people rushing towards me as I drifted away.

I stared at the balcony, estimating its height from the ground. If my plan failed, I could be paralyzed, put into a coma only to wake once more, lose abilities for the rest of the life I was forced to live. I could lose any autonomy I still clung to. It was risky, was it worth it? I tried to calculate my odds of success and lost track of time formulating a plan. What about Brock? He was only thirteen, he would be stuck with the mental image of my disfigured corpse for the rest of his life. It would traumatize everyone involved; it was selfish. As selfish as it was, I was desperate and continued to contemplate the idea. It was an opportunity, and it was right in front of me.

I needed to silence my head before I made any rash decisions. The only thing that quieted it had been taken from me, but I'd been in similar situations before. I needed pain to focus on instead, and I needed it quickly. That night, I pulled the covers over my head to shield it from the prying eyes of Nurse Tina and began to hit myself with the bony portion of my wrist. Over and over again, I pounded the portion of my face by my eye. I could hear the sound of flesh meeting flesh, but the sound of the fans kept it from reaching Nurse Tina. I couldn't stop,

129

I hit myself until the scene faded and continued for a few more minutes for good measure.

By the time I regained control of myself, my face stung, and swelling had decreased my field of vision. I got up to confess what I had done, knowing they would find out in the morning if not then. "Nurse Tina," I called from her doorway. "I hit myself."

She looked at me for a second before yelling, "Kayliegh! Kayliegh!"

Kayliegh came rushing in and I looked at her. She gasped when I turned my face towards her. "Faber, what happened?"

"Is it bad?" I asked innocently. Of course it was bad, any time I lost control of myself it was guaranteed to be bad.

"You have a black eye, kid," she stammered.

"Kayliegh, you'll have to watch him for the rest of the night," Nurse Tina sighed, handing me an icepack. "Keep that on there, do not take it off."

I held the cold pack to my cheek as I laid down once more. I was more at peace, my mind had somewhat quieted. I heard the nurse on the phone with my parents, the nurse practitioner, and therapists, flying from one conversation to the next but I tried to focus on trying to relax. Kayliegh sprawled out in the hallway, watching a show on her computer while she sat by me. I asked to use the bathroom and looked at it in the mirror, it was distinctly swollen with splotches of purple forming within the widespread redness. It didn't look nearly as bad as I had expected it to yet. I used the restroom and went back to my humble cot where I was finally able to fall asleep.

"Woah!" Brock's voice jolted me awake. "What happened to your face?"

I came up with a quick lie while I came to my senses, "I ran into a door."

"Oh, was the nurse's door closed and you didn't notice?" he asked.

I hadn't filled in the gaps of my story yet, so I lazily stole the idea he offered. "Yep. I had my head turned and wasn't paying attention and I ran into it."

"Dude, it looks gnarly!" he laughed as he walked into the vitals room.

I sat up and looked at my reflection on the glass door of the phone booth. It was now a well-defined bruise, covering my entire undereye region and spreading all the way back towards my ear. I sighed, I was in for a long day of therapy and questioning. I went to grab my glasses, only to find out that they had been stepped on and broken while I had been sleeping. I got my vitals taken and tried to avoid smiling as it was always followed by pain and wincing. As usual, they took pictures to document the damage before sending me out to the milieu.

I found Clara lying on the orange couch reading a book and asked her to shower. She did a quick double take when she saw my face but didn't say anything and unlocked the sharps closet to grab my toiletries. In the shower, I was reminded of Michael. *A life sentence.* I began hitting myself again to get rid of the thought. The bruise made it more painful, but after a few strikes, I was able to gather myself and finish washing my hair. I had to hurry as my showers still had a five-minute time limit. I dried off and got dressed, finishing my morning routine.

As I sat down for breakfast, Brock announced, "My new nickname for you is Blackeye."

"No, Brock," Clara scolded. "That's not appropriate, don't call him that."

"Why not?" he whined.

I stayed quiet and ate my hashbrowns and eggs. I wasn't hungry, but you learn quickly to ignore your hunger queues at a place

131

like Pomegranate. Supposedly, it was just a typical part of recovery, you could no longer trust your body to tell you when you're hungry or full. I had learned to push past the twisting of my stomach as I forced food down my throat. Brock clearly had as well, as he had the unfortunate tendency to eat until he was violently ill. His portions were enormous, much larger than mine. His plates were always filled to the brim with food, and he still had to supplement them with daily shakes that mostly consisted of heavy whipping cream. The shakes often turned his face pale, and he wasn't able to finish them without getting sick. I honestly felt bad for him, I'd never seen a person have to eat more than him in my entire life and he was only a little boy.

I spent most of the day listening to Hozier's new album on my iPod while trying to ignore the sequences playing on repeat in my head. Falling, jumping, breaking, dying. Screaming, yelling, crying, sirens. It was extremely graphic, but I slowly grew used to it, and even began to find comfort in the idea that it could all be over so quickly. Someone had previously asked what would happen if a person were to die in the facility so I had knowledge of what the proceedings would be afterwords. Knowledge is equivalent to comfort; peace is found in closure and restlessness in the unknown.

I personally believed in an afterlife, but I had a unique interpretation of it. I believed a person's afterlife would directly reflect what they believed it would be. For example, if a person believed they were going to Heaven, their afterlife would replicate what they believed Heaven to be. Due to this belief, I tried to keep my idea of the afterlife broad and idealistic.

I believed I would live in a flower field, and I would have the body of a normal boy. I would be able to come back to visit Earth through candle flames, enabling my friends to still communicate with me. Of course, I wouldn't be entirely alone either. There would be plentiful animals and lovely people to talk to and make flower crowns for. My blonde hair would be curly rather than straight and I would frolic around the field with a flower crown and vintage pants. I wouldn't wear a shirt, because I would want to show off my flat chest and muscular abdomen. The flowery afterlife I believed in was perfect, but didn't discourage me from picturing my own death, or worse, causing it.

I thought of my friends, and I felt that I owed it to them to at least attempt to save myself. That night, as KV was about to leave, I asked her if we could talk in the family room. The lights were flickering, and a storm was raging outside. This was the weather I had decided I wanted to die in years prior, but I couldn't think of a reasonable excuse to go on the balcony in this weather, so I knew I wouldn't be able to follow through with my plan that day. KV and I began closing the windows together to dampen the howling sound the wind was producing before we talked.

Finally, KV sat across from me and asked, "What did you want to talk about?"

I had to be honest, for my friends' sake, I had to at least try. "How do you stop yourself from wanting to die? I keep picturing it in my head, planning it. I don't know how to make it stop."

"Faber, do you know why I became a therapist?" she pondered. I shook my head. "My best friend in college committed suicide. It changed my entire world; I'll never forget it. I know it's hard to believe, but there are people who love you beyond belief and want you on this Earth. Your friends, they'll never forget it. They'll never be able to fill your space, they'll never forgive themselves for not saving you, they'll never fully be able to understand why it happened."

"I've been gone for so long, it seems best to do it now. They're used to me not being there, they're used to not hearing my voice. They don't even make time to talk to me. Now is the best time, they're as separated from me as they're ever going to be. Nothing will change for them," I reasoned.

"Everything will change for them," she replied. "Right now, they think you're coming home. They're comfortable because they believe you're safe and they believe you're coming home. Knowing you aren't coming home will change everything."

"They don't care!" I cried. "I sit in the phone booth every single day, dialing their numbers. I've done it so many times I know their phone numbers by heart now. I sit there and call again and again, every night. Every night I walk out of the phone booth on the verge of tears because they didn't pick up. Every night. They don't care anymore."

"Faber, they care. I promise you, they care. I know it hurts but this is the busiest time of the year for them. They're living their lives and I'm sure they think of you all the time. Listen, you are so special. You're talented, you're kind, you're patient, you're funny. You are truly an unforgettable person, and you cannot end your life early. It is not your time. Come with me to my car, I'll give you a hair tie to snap on your wrist to help ground you and magazines to tear up. You're going to get through this."

I followed her into the garage and walked with her to her pristine white van. She dug around in the backseat before handing me a hair tie and a thick magazine. I thanked her and put the black elastic around my wrist and returned to the milieu as she left for the night. Brock and Jessie, another tech, sat together watching TV in the dim room. They were watching an old Disney movie, one of Brock's favorite genres.

Jessie tended to be a bit harsh and often over-portioned food, causing her to be widely disliked. I didn't mind her all that much, I didn't specifically like her, but I didn't dislike her either. She had a lot of things going on in her life, it made sense to me why she was the way she was. She was dealing with infertility and going through treatments that had been unsuccessful up to that point. It was emotionally tolling on her, and sometimes it showed. The art of being a people pleaser is that nobody ever knows if I dislike them unless I want them to and because of that, we were mutually respectful and kind to each other. Brock on the other hand, had a talent for pushing her to her limits and they were often volatile towards each other.

I sat in my spot and began writing a new letter to Bronwyn, this one with a purpose.

Dear Bronwyn,

It feels like I'm never going to see you again. I'm really struggling right now. I'm very suicidal to be completely honest. If there was a way for me to fall asleep and not wake up completely painlessly right now, I would do it. Sometimes, I feel as though the safety here is almost inhumane as it's prolonging my suffering.

If anything happens, my phone password is 3572 and the password for all my emails and everything else is either MapFan99 or MapFan99! (try both). I hope nothing happens because I want to see you, Daisy, and Callie again more than anything but it's just growing more and more tempting and pain is becoming less of a deterrent.

I've written better suicide letters to you (there's one in the notes app of my phone) but this one is just in case. I want you to know how much I appreciate you. You taught me what true empathy, understanding, and comfort looks and feels like. You modeled kindness and acceptance to me. You are driven, smart, funny, hardworking, talented, beautiful, and so much more. I don't think you'll ever know how much you mean to me. You are a better friend than I ever deserved or could have asked for.

I miss you so much and I love you more than anything <3

Your friend,

Faber Elliott

I finished writing exactly one minute before it was time to prepare evening snack. I knew I would write another note, that was the worst suicide note I had written in my entire life, and I'd written many, but for the time being it put me at ease. At the very least, if I did anything too impulsive, I had something written down on paper, something to let her know that I still cared and I had thought of her. I followed Jessie and Brock into the kitchen to prepare a snack with them and sat down at the large wooden table in the dining room to eat. I wasn't hungry, but it didn't matter anymore. I was positive I would be dead in a matter of weeks if not days, nothing mattered.

The topic of conversation that night was fast food establishments. The conversation was innocent at first until Brock stated, "I like Chick-Fil-A the best. My grandma donates money to them."

Jessie's expression shifted immediately. "Brock!" she chastised. "That's wildly inappropriate!"

"What do you mean?" he yelled back.

"Do you know the horrible things they stand for? The only reason you would donate money to them is to hurt the LGBTQ community!" she accused.

"That's not true! That isn't why we donate money to them!" he insisted. I sat quietly, not daring to interrupt or try to diffuse the situation. I began to snap the hair tie on my wrist in distress to keep myself calm. Each snap brought a sharp sting and a jolt of mild pain, it felt wonderful.

"What other reason could there possibly be?" she shot back.

"We don't support abortion!" he screamed.

There was a split second of shock induced silence, before Jessie shouted, "That's it, snack is over!" She sprang up from the table, taking Brock's shake with her and went into the kitchen shouting a string of profanities. Brock had struck a nerve, and I was once again along for the ride.

We weren't supposed to be left unattended; we were obligated to stay within her line of sight. I turned to Brock, "Let's go."

I picked up my dishes and led him into the kitchen where Jessie yelled, "Brock go to the nurse's station, I don't even want to look at you right now!"

He obliged and I was left sitting in the kitchen with Jessie. I snapped the elastic on my wrist harder and quicker to help soothe my anxiety. I awkwardly asked, "Should I go to the nurse's station too to give you some time?"

"No, Faber, you're always a delight to have around," she replied. "I just can't handle Brock, he drives me crazy. I could just..." she motioned smacking him. "Of course, I won't." She began to cry. "I'm going to lose my job! I'm going to lose my job because of that little brat!"

"I'm sure you won't lose your job," I tried to console her. I didn't want to sit there and comfort her when my own anxiety was so high, but what choice did I have? I could feel my wrist stinging with each release of the hair tie.

Brock walked back into the kitchen, "I still have to complete my shake."

Jessie slammed it down onto the counter in front of him, "How do you believe that, Brock? You really believe women should have no choice over what they do with their bodies? How could you believe something so evil?"

"I respect your opinion, I just disagree," Brock reasoned.

"Well I can't respect your opinion at all because it's just evil!" Jessie slapped back.

I walked over to the nurse's station as Jessie continued yelling at Brock and took my medications. It was time for my phone call and I dialed Bronwyn's number through muscle memory alone. I expected to hear her voicemail again, but was surprised to here, "Hello?" in Bronwyn's voice instead.

"Bronwyn! Thank god!" I exclaimed. "Bronwyn, I have to tell you something, but I have to whisper it, ok?"

"Is everything ok?" her voice spiked anxiously.

"For now, yes, I'm safe. I'm going to be honest with you though, I'm really not doing well. I'm so depressed and miserable, it's bad again."

"Do you know how much longer you'll be there?" she tried.

"No idea. Listen, if I stop calling, do you promise me that you'll be ok?" I asked.

"Faber, no. Please, I miss you," she bargained.

"It's ok, it's all going to be ok. I have to go now, I'm sorry," I muttered quickly.

"I love you."

"I love you too," I assured her. "Goodbye."

"I love you," she insisted. I could hear Jessie and Brock still fighting in the background.

"I love you too." I hung up the phone as she began to say it again to change my mind. Nothing was going to change my mind; it was too late.

The yelling didn't stop until Brock was in bed, and by that time I was tired enough to go to bed as well. I didn't want to be alone with Jessie any longer. The way she had screamed had reminded me of my own home and I didn't want to be her shoulder to cry on when she was supposed to be mine. I got into bed and continued slapping my wrist with the hair tie until Jessie came over.

"Faber, what are you doing?" she asked. "Let me see your wrist."

138

"KV gave it to me, she said I could!" I argued.

"Let me see your wrists," Jessie insisted. I held it up to her, seeing it myself for the first time. It was red and bruised, with little splotches of purple pinpointing where the band had made contact. "Give it to me," Jessie ordered.

"No! KV gave it to me!" I cried.

"Give it to me, Faber. I'll call KV and if she says you can keep it, I'll give it back, but it looks like you've taken it too far," she compromised. It was her fault I had taken it too far; I had been stressed because of her the entire evening.

It wasn't fair, but I gave it to her anyways. I got a sudden spike of anxiety, "Am I in trouble?"

She walked away to call Kendall, returning a few minutes later. "You can't have it back, but KV said to tell you that you are absolutely not in trouble." She gave me a hug and walked away to let me go to sleep. We weren't allowed to hug. It wasn't fair that out of all the people here who could have hugged me, it had to be the one person whose hug offered me no comfort.

As I laid there, picturing my intentional death once more, an idea struck me. I could overdose, it would be far easier and less traumatic for those involved. The medications were locked up in the nurse's office, but I could pretend to take the ones they gave me and hide them away. After a while, I would surely have enough to overdose. I would have to take far more pills than I had on my first attempt, at least twenty, maybe thirty. Hiding away two to three pills a day would allow me to attempt in less than two weeks. It was a foolproof idea, a genius plan. In the meantime, if I had an opportunity to jump, I would.

The next afternoon, after lunch, Reya walked in and asked, "Faber, can we talk?"

"Sure," I responded. Reya wasn't my therapist, but her presence gave me so much comfort that I was more than happy to meet with her instead. She took me into the family room and gently prompted, "Kendall told me you've been having suicidal thoughts, can you tell me a bit about them?"

"I guess scenes just play on a loop in my mind. Scenes of me killing myself, and I want to do it," I explained.

"How would you do it, Faber?" she asked.

I thought for a minute before deciding to be vague, but still provide enough detail to tell my friends that I tried to fix things. "Well, a few weeks ago, I drew a picture of me hanging myself in the closet. I could hang myself with something, or I could jump off of something high." I purposefully excluded my idea about stashing pills, not wanting to give that brilliant idea away.

"You've been writing a lot lately, is this why?" she delved further.

"I've written a lot of letters, but they're just in case. I want my friends to know that I still care, that I thought of them. The only reason I'm telling you this is because I owe it to them to at least try to save myself. I love them so much and Bronwyn..." I trailed off. Bronwyn had cried when she just thought about losing me, I couldn't make her cry again. On the other hand, it would be the final time I ever hurt Bronwyn, she would never have to worry about me again. I changed what I was about to say, "Bronwyn would be proud of me for telling you."

"I'm sure she would be," Reya agreed. "It really is concerning that you're writing letters though. Listen Faber, you have so much life ahead of you to live. Situations are temporary, you're going to be such an important person in this world. You can't leave yet."

I gave her the same argument I had given KV about my friends not caring as much anymore. I might as well be dead to them. I wasn't there and had almost no way to talk to them. It really was the best opportunity I would ever have to slip away quietly, to cause the least distress possible. It could be days, even weeks, before they even heard about it. They wouldn't be concerned by my absence at school, it was already explained. In theory, they could live the rest of their lives never even knowing that I had died. They could simply think I was still in treatment or had transferred schools once I got back.

"Why do you want to die?" Reya asked desperately. There were so many reasons, I couldn't even begin to list them all.

"I once heard a quote from a movie that dying was like slipping into a warm bath. I like to think of it that way. I like to imagine that the comfort of death just embraces you. It seems so comfortable, so quiet, so peaceful." I could feel my body begin to relax just from describing it. Reya and I talked a bit more, before she sent me back to the milieu with the instructions not to write any more letters.

Of course, I immediately wrote more letters, I was in a fury of determination. I had to get everything done before I died, I had to make sure I was ready to leave. I wrote letters to my favorite staff members from the facility in the blue notebook I had been given as it was the one they were most likely to look through. Writing suicide letters came easily to me, I had done it many times. My style for these letters was different than my typical writing style. I didn't want to be overly philosophical or paint myself as a martyr, I tried to write them in the same fashion in which I talked. I wanted the readers of these letters to be able to hear my voice speaking to them when they read the letters, so they were kept quite casual. Suicide is no occasion to be flashy, it's an occasion for everyone involved to be empathetic.

That night, when I went to take my medications, I decided to put my grand plan into action. Using sleight of hand, I pretended to take the pills while I dropped them down into my sleeve. I then placed my hand into my pocket and let the pills fall safely into it. The nurse didn't catch me, and I felt elated. I asked to use the restroom and Kayleigh forgot to check my pockets. I knew she would correct her mistake when I came out, so I wrapped the pills in a strip of toilet paper and shoved them into the small pocket inside of the main pocket of my jeans. I successfully made it through the pocket checks and made a mental note to put the pills in the same pocket moving forward to avoid getting caught.

Every Friday was family visitation day, with family therapy held on that day as well. On the Friday before Easter, Brock began acting a bit suspicious. He was able to request an extra hour of school time, took surveys on the facility iPad, and had his belongings checked. He assured me that this was a standard procedure if you stayed in the facility for an abnormally long time. I believed him hesitantly. After all, he had arrived at the facility in November, and it was now April. Everyone in the facility gathered on the couch before family therapy time and I got a distinct feeling of dread. Reya popped up on the TV through a Zoom call and exclaimed, "Happy Graduation Day, Brock! You didn't think I would miss it, did you?"

I felt a lump in my throat but shoved it down. For the last month, Brock had been the only person even close to a friend I had. We had lived together for two months; he was like a little brother to me. He couldn't graduate! I would be so alone, there were no other kids in the entire facility. I remembered the screams of a girl in the psychiatric triage of the ER, "No! I can't go to treatment! I'll be so alone! I'll be so lonely!" I felt the same panic as her, but rather than screaming it, I held it down.

We passed around Brock's bracelet and shared our favorite quotes he had said before he put his handprint on the tree with the number of days he had been at the facility, 131, painted underneath it. I was able to fight the tears during the ceremony, but I could feel the mask slipping and sat down to independently color. KV sat next to me and asked, "Are you ok, Faber?"

I came undone, tears began streaming down my face as I whimpered, "I don't want to see my family today!" I was going to die soon; I didn't want to see them. Brock would leave in only a few hours, and I would no longer have to worry about scaring him. Once I had enough pills, I would surely carry out my plan.

"Aw, are you crying over me?" Brock asked sincerely.

142

"Among other things," I bawled. Never once had I cried in front of people in this facility besides during family therapy alone with my parents and KV. Cendall had urged me before to allow my emotions to show, worrying about my invincible exterior. I refused to cry in front of adults unless it was out of my control, and in that moment, it was. I sat on the floor by the couch sniffling and gasping for air. Andrea looked at me in surprise, only for a second. There were so many reasons to cry. I was about to break my family's heart, but they had already broken mine.

The doorbell rang and I began to sob harder while KV ushered my parents downstairs quickly. I hadn't even stopped crying before I was made to follow behind them to spend an hour of time together. They had brought Easter gifts and I opened them while crying. Cendall and KV entered the room and began the family therapy session. Typically, only KV did family therapy, but supposedly the topics we were supposed to discuss that day were important enough for Cendall to join us. I sat silently as my parents talked, coloring on a piece of paper while tears traced my face.

"Faber," Cendall interrupted, "I've never seen you like this. What's going on?"

"I don't want to see my parents!" I insisted.

"I feel like you're being unfair to them," KV accused.

"It isn't my fault," I said quietly, focusing still on the coloring page in front of me.

"What do you mean?" KV asked.

I took a deep breath, I hadn't told anyone this part of the story yet. "Michael, he didn't want me to be close to my parents. I think his reasoning for that is pretty obvious. I was already having issues at home as it was, but he taught me how to ignore them. He taught me how to act like my parents didn't even exist and told me it would fix things. I've been manually hardwired to not want to be around my parents. It isn't my fault."

A silence followed, a long painful silence. I was able to stop crying after I admitted that. The flow of tears ceased, and I felt a sense of relief.

"It all makes sense now," KV remarked. "Everything makes so much sense. That's terrible, Faber. I can see how this man has hurt you and your family."

Whatever topics had been planned for the day were dismissed and the rest of the session was spent discussing Michael and what he had taught me to do. I remained quieter than usual but felt a new sense of neutrality. I had explained myself and part of the reason I pushed my parents away so hard. Of course, there were other reasons, but the explanation I had given would suffice for now. I felt able to disappear in peace once more, like one more thing had been checked off of my end-of-life bucket list.

Brock left that afternoon, and the following day was designated as a self-care day for me. It wasn't so bad being alone after all, at least not in the beginning. We played Taylor Swift loudly in the background as we did crafts, facemasks, and I braided Clara and Raven's hair. I even got to cut my hair for the first time in months under KV and Cendall's supervision. For a moment, it felt as though the entire world revolved around me. Of course, it came crashing down the second my phone calls were ignored once more. Still, I kept a happy face. It wouldn't matter soon, nothing would. For now, I was the king and for the rest of my short life, I would be invincible.

I continued collecting pills every night, stashing them all in the small pocket of that pair of jeans. I brought the jeans into the bathroom with me when I showered, along with another pair, claiming I didn't know which ones to wear. I always returned the ones with the pills neatly to my drawer after putting on the second pair of pants I had picked out. I was caught once with a pill in my sleeve, but I told the nurse I had accidentally dropped it and put it into my mouth, hiding it in my cheek. I ran to the bathroom, wrapped it in toilet paper, and placed it in my pocket before it had time to dissolve in my cheek. I began hiding all of the pills in my cheek after that, in a place that was hidden when they told me to open my mouth for them to check and ensure I had taken the medications. My sneakiness prevailed, and the pills quickly began to add up.

As the days went by, staff members remarked that they had never seen me happier. I had all the reasons in the world to be happy, my plan was working, and I could see the end. I stopped hitting myself and picking at my fingers, the old habits were trivial now. I was even able to sleep in my room, in a bed, for the first time as a reward for good behavior. It made it even easier to hide the pills. Once the door had been closed, I would creep to the dresser to hide them in the small pocket of the folded jeans. I slept peacefully, relenting to the minute death we call sleep.

The day before I planned to attempt, I wrote Bronwyn a new letter:

Dear Bronwyn,

I miss you so so much and I really hope that everything is going well for you. I sent another note for you in shorthand, the translation key is in the back of the journal I made for you. Just hang onto it, it will make sense later. I would give absolutely anything to give you a hug right now. If you walked through the door, I would never let you go. God, I miss you. I miss the heavenly sounds of choir, the intensity of mock trial, getting peace signs from you, absolutely everything.

I'm working on more letters to send to you, and I know you're really busy, but it would absolutely make my week if you had time to send a letter back. I'm the only client here right now by the way, the other client left, and I cried so hard. He was like a little brother to me. As many bad things

145

as he said, he could also be so genuine, and I seriously loved the little guy.

I listened to Taylor Swift all day today. I love her now, she reminds me of you, Daisy, Belle, and Emilia. A big weight has been lifted off my chest recently and my therapists said they've never seen me so happy so that's good.

I can't wait to hear from you and I miss you so much! <3333333333333

Yours truly,

Faber Elliott

The note I had written to her in shorthand was the real letter I intended to send her. I had written it in characters representing letters and numbers that I had created myself to ensure nobody else would be able to read it. It offered an explanation as to why I wanted to die so desperately. KV had mentioned possibly reporting my father to CPS again, after I recounted an incident that had happened a year prior to her. I had to die before my family found out, it was just one reason of many. I wrote them all out in a shorthand list for her, pleading for her to understand. She had to understand.

When I was finished, I turned to Clara, "Can you please come into work tomorrow, Clara? Please, it's really important."

"Maybe, I don't know if I'll be able to get up in time," she resisted.

"It doesn't matter, you can come in late, you just have to be there. Please," I begged. She shrugged her shoulders and Raven took over her place in the milieu while she walked out for her break. I figured that was the best response I would be able to get and decided not to push it any further. I still had some bases to cover before I went through with my plan the following morning, so I turned to Raven next.

"Raven," I asked, "What would happen if there were no clients here anymore? Hypothetically?"

"I suppose we would probably just do some team building exercises and training," she responded nonchalantly. "Why?"

"No reason," I lied. "But everything would be ok? You'd still get paid and everything?"

"Probably, we've always had at least one client here since we've opened so it's hard to say for sure," she informed me. That was enough reassurance for me to feel at ease.

"Can I have a hug?" I pleaded.

"You know we aren't allowed to," she responded. "Don't ask Clara or Kayliegh either, you know none of us are allowed to. I'm sorry."

"Okay," I sighed. I tried once more to give Clara and Raven a hug before they left for the day, my requests were denied.

I called Bronwyn one last time to tell her goodbye forever. She didn't pick up and I nearly cried but held it together. I needed to tell her goodbye, I had to hear her say it back. It had shattered my soul that she hadn't been able to say it on our last call. "I love you" doesn't provide the same closure as "goodbye." I asked Kayleigh for a hug before bed, reasoning that Jessie had given me one. She told me no and turned off the lights, leaving me alone with my thoughts once again.

Chapter Thirteen: Can You See Me?

"Suicide is a form of murder - premeditated murder. It isn't something you do the first time you think of doing it. It takes getting used to. And you need the means, the opportunity, the motive. A successful suicide demands good organization and a cool head, both of which are usually incompatible with the suicidal state of mind."

-Susanna Kaysen

At last, the day came I had been waiting for, April 20, 2023. Clara didn't show up, it was just me and Raven. I was mildly upset, I wanted to spend my final day with both Raven and Clara. It was the closest I could get to spending it with my friends. I thought about how Bronwyn hadn't answered, how I'd never get to say goodbye to her, how desperately Daisy had tried to convince me not to go through with my plan. It didn't matter, I didn't want to live to see another day. I couldn't handle the disappointment of waking up to see another morning.

I grabbed the pair of jeans I had hidden the pills in and brought it into the bathroom with me. Raven sat outside my door as usual, but I didn't have to talk to her while I showered anymore. I dumped the pills into my hand and counted them one last time, thirty pills. I got in the shower and washed myself carefully and slowly, making sure to reach every inch of my body. I held the pills in one hand away from the water. My heart began to pound as I let the water fill my mouth and dumped half the pills into it. I took nearly the rest of the pills in another quick gulp, leaving just a few to put back in my pocket to explain my sudden death if I didn't have time to confess. I turned off the water and got dressed before shakily opening the door and finishing getting ready.

I decided to email my friends reluctantly. I wanted to tell them goodbye, I really cared about them, but I was nearly bitter that they hadn't answered when nothing else could have mattered more in the world. I didn't want to come off as dramatic or purposely scare them, so I crafted the most optimistic and simplistic email I could think of and sent it to Taylor, Bronwyn, and Daisy.

Hello, I'm really really sorry but I just tried to overdose and took a bunch of stuff so I won't be calling for a while. It probably won't work but I'll probably have to go to the hospital again. Love you all so much.

I logged out of my email and followed Raven to the kitchen to prepare breakfast, leaning on counters and tables to hide the shakiness that I couldn't suppress. We brought the smoothies to the table and Raven sat across from me. She slowly began to eat her smoothie, but I didn't follow her example. I sat without moving, only looking at the smoothie sitting in front of me.

Raven looked at me with a concerned expression, "What's wrong?"

I smiled nervously, "Nothing."

"You never refuse like this. Is it something I said? Did something in the shower trigger you? Was it something someone else said? Is it because you couldn't talk to your friends?" I shook my head in response to each question, wishing I could wipe the smile off my face.

"Everything is fine." I assured her, laying my head on the table briefly.

She looked at me with a concerned expression, clearly trying to figure out what was wrong. "Would you eat cereal?"

"No, I can't eat right now," I responded.

"But you love cereal..." she said almost pitifully.

I wanted comfort, but we weren't allowed to touch. I was so scared of any pain that was to come. I reached for her, placing two of my fingers on the table in front of her. She slowly touched two of her fingers to the tops of my fingertips. I was comforted and for a moment we sat like that while she analyzed my face. Finally, she got up and poured us both a supplement, hoping that if she drank with me, I would complete it. I still didn't eat or drink, I was far too anxious to. As we sat at the table, I continued to silently seek a calming touch by touching her fingers.

I swallowed two more pills when her back was turned before heading down to school. I silently began to work, but the pills quickly caught up to me. I lost chunks of time, only returning to reality when the teacher scolded me for not working. I felt an overwhelming sense of fatigue and began to shake. After another scolding I turned to Raven desperately, "I really need to take a nap now. I'm done with school today."

"No, you need to stay here and work," she replied.

I turned back towards my computer, feeling ill. After a few minutes, I turned to Raven again, "Can I go to the bathroom?"

She got up and I followed her, tripping on the stairs and falling. I got up and made my way to the bathroom only to lie down on the floor without even closing the door. I was dangerously close to passing out, and I couldn't have stood upright any longer. I waited for the feeling to pass while Raven came and sat beside me.

"Listen," I moaned. "I took a bunch of pills this morning and I'm really not feeling well. I can't do anymore school."

"You're really pale," she remarked quietly. "You don't look well at all. Do you think you can use the bathroom without passing out?"

I stood up slowly, assuring her that I could, and let her leave while I used the restroom. I caught a glimpse of my face in the mirror, it had gone completely ashen, the only color left was the dark circles that stained the area underneath my eyes. When I came out, I was taken up to the nurse's station where the nurse took my vitals and I handed over the rest of the pills I had pocketed to prove that I was being truthful.

My memory was fleeting at this point, I can only remember the following events. I was taken to lay on the orange couch and I began to lose track of time. I had my scheduled meeting with my psychiatrist where I lied, assuring him I was fine as I fought to stay conscious. The meeting was short, as usual, and I was grateful to return to the couch to rest. I was surprised that I was expected to carry on with my day, but relieved that I was able to stay, and hopefully die, in the comfort of this home.

I went to my nutrition meeting after a bit of resting and a few medications to fight the nausea that had begun to creep up on me. There was a new nutritionist, Parker, who was training. It was her first time leading a nutrition meeting and I really hoped to push past everything to make it easy for her. Unfortunately, all hopes cannot become a reality and I could no longer pretend I was alright.

I laid on the much smaller, blue velvet couch in the hexagonal room and attempted to listen. There was something on my legs, I had to move them. I kicked around restlessly, fighting invisible entities. I slipped in and out of consciousness, waking only to kick around once more. I tried to stay awake, I fought to open my eyes, but they wouldn't open. I could hear voices in fleeting moments, only for them to disappear into nothingness once more.

"Faber, are you alright?" a voice asked.

"Yes, I'm fine." I responded.

"Faber? Faber?"

Hadn't I answered? Perhaps the words never touched my lips and they had only formed in my head. A variety of questions passed in this manner, I made them out and responded, only to realize I hadn't actually responded before slipping out of consciousness once more. I may have slurred some syllables together, I'm not entirely sure. I was unable to hear my own voice, only my inner dialogue responded to the words that reached my ears. Eventually, I was led back to the orange couch in the milieu where I fell into another dreamless sleep.

I only remember waking up twice this time. The first time, Kendall stood over me and informed me in a melancholy tone that they were planning on creating a prom day for me to make up for the fact that I missed my own. The staff had brought dresses to work and were going to allow me to do their hair. I was told it would be moved to a later date as I was clearly incapacitated. *That's so sweet*, I thought, but the words likely never left my mouth before I was asleep once more.

 I opened my eyes for a brief moment to see Reya standing over me. Her expression was that of pure concern as she looked into my eyes and quietly asked, "Can you see me?" This time, even I didn't hear an answer before the world faded once more.

"Faber, we're calling an ambulance." Cendall's voice echoed from above me. I groggily fought to sit up and stay awake as I waited silently. "Don't worry, we made sure you won't go to MidPoint again. It's going to be okay this time, okay?"

I was beyond the point of responding, I just sat there as people rushed around me. The ambulance showed up quickly and soon EMTs were putting stickers with metal buttons on them all over me. I tried to help them but was too slow and clumsy to be any help. They told me the stickers were for my heart because of the medicines I had taken. Before I even got onto the ambulance, a plethora of wires were connected to me. This was clearly far more serious than my first ambulance ride.

I was taken into the ambulance and Raven sat in the seat Clara had once occupied. The EMT placed an IV in me and started running IV fluids. I didn't feel the pain, I couldn't feel anything. Raven looked so terrified and sat so quietly, I wanted to make her laugh. I tried to say something funny but wasn't even aware of the words I spoke and was soon unconscious for the remainder of the ambulance ride.

When we arrived, I briefly awoke as I was rolled into the Emergency Room. I could hear nurses remarking that there was nothing they could do since I had taken the pills so long ago as I passed them in the hallway. I was either going to live or die, I still held out hope for the latter. I never wanted to go home again, to hear my deadname again, to be seen as a girl again, to be separated from my friends again, to hear another word this vile world had to offer, or to pray to an entity that didn't exist out of pure desperation. I wanted to die surrounded by people who saw me as a boy, who were unable to hide their concern for me despite their efforts, who would surely remember me as Faber Elliott regardless of what name ended up on my gravestone.

The room I was taken to was as empty as I expected it to be except this time there wasn't even a bed, only a large green armchair propped against a wall. I changed into paper scrubs while I was still awake, forest green ones this time, and then draped myself sideways across the armchair.

Raven glanced at me and softly said, "Clara says hi."

Clara, I wished Clara was here as well. I had asked her to come into work, I wanted her to be with me too. I don't remember if I mumbled a reply before falling asleep again despite the terrible discomfort of my position on the chair.

The next time I awoke, Raven was still sitting across from me talking on the phone and I nurse was pulling out my IV. She instructed me to follow her and I obliged, not bidding Raven goodbye. I was entirely numb, I didn't know where I was going, nor did I care. I was led to a holding cell of sorts. A miniscule brick hallway with two openings for doors on each side, the door was locked behind me and on the other end of the hallway was a large glass window where a nurse sat to observe the inhabitants. Three other boys sat on small plastic chairs they had set up in the middle of the hallway talking loudly.

"And I have three felonies!" a stocky young boy bragged.

A lanky, pink haired boy stifled a laugh as a blond boy with absent eyes responded, "My schizophrenia was acting up, that's what got me here. Why are you here?"

All eyes shifted towards me as I sat on top of a plastic nightstand someone had dragged out of their room. "I tried to overdose." A somber silence followed. "Which room is mine? I'm going to go to bed."

"That one," the pink haired boy replied pointing to the room labeled "1." "You won't be able to sleep with us talking though."

"Yeah, we're pretty loud," the stocky boy said, making no offer to quiet down.

I could already feel the heavy pull of sleep overcoming me again, "I'm pretty sure I'll manage."

I walked into the room and laid on the plastic mattress. The bed was nearly identical to the ones at MidPoint, beside it stood another plastic nightstand. A TV encased in wood and plexiglass was mounted on the wall across from me, playing an obnoxiously loud show. The lights remained on and the boys continued to converse. Despite this, I had no problem falling asleep.

"They have a place for you at Hyfield!" a nurse exclaimed to wake me up. The lights were off now, the voices in the hallway had ceased, the TV still played. I rolled out of bed silently and followed her out of the holding cell. I was taken to another driver with the same chipper attitude the last one had possessed. I glanced at the clock, becoming aware of the time for the first time since the morning I overdosed, it was now 1:32 the next morning. It was pitch black outside, but the drive wasn't long. Only a few winding paths separated the main hospital and its psychiatric counterpart, Hyfield.

I was taken up to the adolescent unit where the night staff greeted me. "Would you like anything to drink?"

"Can I have a diet coke?" I asked hopefully.

"I'm sorry we don't have that," the nurse replied. I responded that I was alright in that case and allowed them to proceed with the admittance process. I was taken into a padded room where I was strip searched before being led down the hallway to my room. My roommate was already asleep in the dark room and mumbled a greeting as the nurse introduced us. Roxy, the roommate, shifted under her covers as I crawled into mine and waited to fall asleep.

The next morning, I woke up to find my clothes waiting for me in the bottom of the cubby in our room. *I don't have to earn my clothes?* I rushed into the bathroom, which was only separated from the room by a curtain attached to a rod in the ceiling by Velcro, to change into the clothes. I only received my shirt and socks as my pants and hoodie had strings, but I was elated that I didn't have to work for them. I put the soft socks underneath the grip filled ones we were required to wear and threw away the scrub shirt after replacing it with my tie-dye t-shirt.

I walked out into the open living space and found the table with my name taped to it before sitting down. "Do you want breakfast?" a nurse asked.

"No thanks," I responded, unused to the freedom of choosing when or what to eat.

I heard a few kids talking about someone named Autumn, asking where she was. I ignored them and asked the front desk for my toiletries. I was given them, and I went back to my room to shower and brush my teeth and hair. I was surprised to learn that our rooms remained unlocked, and we were allowed to use the restroom, take a nap, or simply retreat for a little while whenever we pleased. My roommate took full advantage of this and laid in the bed closest to the window sleeping as I slipped into the shower. The water was nice and warm, and I carefully poured the soap out of the paper cups and lathered it.

When I had finished, I put my shirt and scrub pants back on and dropped my towel off in front of the laundry room door before going back into the living area. There was a girl I hadn't seen yet at the front desk requesting toiletries. She had long black hair, but her roots exposed her natural blonde shade. She had a nose piercing as well as several others and looked rather edgy. She hadn't received her clothes yet, but she still wielded an odd charisma.

155

"Let me see your bracelet," the nurse at the desk told her. I caught a glimpse of the typed name. This was the Autumn everyone had been whispering about. She took her toiletries and headed back to her room without a word, disappearing once more.

A tech floated around the tables and stopped when she reached me, "Aren't you hungry?" she asked.

"No," I replied defensively. "Can I have a notebook to write stuff in?"

"We don't have any here, I can get you a packet of paper though," she offered. I accepted her offer and she quickly came back with a booklet of paper that had somehow been held together in the corner without the use of a staple.

I spent a few minutes decorating the cover page, adorning it with stars and planets and writing my name in large letters. I had nearly recovered fully from my attempt, but I was still dizzy and slightly out of it and everything sounded muffled. The walls of the facility had the lyrics to "What a Wonderful World" wrapping around them, it reminded me of performing it in choir the year prior. It was cold, but not nearly as frigid as MidPoint so I tried not to complain while I curled up in my chair.

I wrote a letter to Bronwyn in the journal using the bendy pen I had been provided in between talking to various doctors, nurses, and social workers. There was nothing else to do, so I laid in my room for a while before returning for the mandated group therapy sessions. I Dutch braided my roommate's hair and was even able to sneak Autumn into my room and braid her hair as well. It gave us the opportunity to talk and we immediately bonded. I knew I would spend the majority of my stay at Hyfield hanging out with her. She was angry to be there and worried about socializing with the other kids, but something about our opposite energies connected us silently.

My parents visited but I was hardly in the mood to talk. I still wished my attempt had worked and seeing them only reminded me that it hadn't. I tried to stay amicable, but it was nearly impossible and I eventually asked them to leave. They brought my glasses, which had finally been fixed. Being able to see clearly almost made their insufferable visit and terrible timing worth it.

A loud alarm went off in the hallway and I ran to my room to lessen the sound only to find that it was locked. All the other doors were still open, which confused me. I found my roommate in the living area and tried to figure out what was going on, "Roxy, why is our room locked?"

She looked up at me with hollow eyes, "They locked it because I was throwing up my food."

"On accident or on purpose?" I pressed. I loved having the freedom of an unlocked room and this new inconvenience left me with little empathy for Roxy.

"On purpose, I told them," she answered. Being placed with a roommate who also suffered from an eating disorder would be detrimental to me, but I was too confused to care.

"Why would you tell them? Don't you want to go home? You're supposed to pretend to be better!" I cried. These were the rules of the psych ward, keep your head down, don't tell them anything they don't already know, put on a happy face, and leave. It seemed simple to me, but clearly Roxy was not on the same page.

"This is my third time here. I really need help and I'm not going home until I get it," she replied. In theory, this response was admirable, but they can only hold you for so long, so I doubted it would yield the results she was seeking.

I scoffed as the alarm sound ended and went to take my pills before bed. I took them and handed the cup to the nurse at the desk but she stopped me from leaving. She got out a flashlight and made me move my tongue and cheeks around to expose the entire inside of my mouth. "I've heard about your notorious pocketing abilities," she remarked before I went back to my seat. I felt an odd sense of accomplishment, sneakiness is nearly synonymous with intelligence.

157

Soon, it was time for bed, and I got up to follow the rest of the kids down the hallway before I was stopped by a tech. "You aren't allowed to go to your room until an hour after you take your medications. We can't have you throwing them up."

At this point, I was absolutely exasperated and sat in the dark area alone for another thirty minutes before I was finally allowed to rest. It was nearly impossible to sleep, the rooms were cold, my roommate was loud, I could hear my heartbeat with my ear pressed against the pillow, and checks were done with a flashlight every fifteen minutes. Even so, sleep eventually found its way to me once more and I was able to rest.

The next morning, I began a new letter to Bronwyn in my makeshift notebook filling her in:

Saturday April 22nd

Dear Bronwyn,

Today we have been separated by biological sex, so I'm in the girls' room. People in the adult ward randomly scream here sometimes which is a little scary. This place is pretty mind numbing and awful to live in but it's still better than MidPoint so I'm trying to stay patient and wait out my stay. I'm on day two out of 3-8 days so that's not too horrible I guess. I can only hope to go home sooner rather than later.

The nurses brought in a rolling TV and allowed us to listen to some music on it through YouTube. We listened to a bit of Melanie Martinez, ROAR, and Twenty-One Pilots before our time with the TV had ended and it was rolled into the main living area where the other boys sat. I sat next to Autumn and talked to her about how ridiculous the separation was. Normally, I would fight to be placed with the boys, but I would have rather talked to Autumn than any of them. We had taken no time to become extremely close. She helped me get away with not eating by eating some of my food for me when the nurses weren't

158

looking, and in return I entertained her by drawing her pictures and telling her stories about Pomegranate.

Once I got bored, I went to my room and began to do pushups and handstands since I had no movement restrictions at Hyfield. I hadn't eaten since before I had been admitted, but the effects of it hadn't reached me yet. I laid down in my bed for a while before showering and getting ready. I observed the writing covering the plastic bases of the bed, all of which was very entertaining. There were a few words of encouragement tangled in with odd poems about monsters and statements of anguish. The entire base was covered in writing and drawings done with crayons. It reminded me of children writing on walls, I suppose for some people the desire to draw on surfaces perpendicular to the floor never left.

A nurse interrupted my exploration, "Time to get your blood drawn, buddy. Wait, what are you doing?"

"Reading the writing down here," I replied from my crouched position.

"I don't recommend doing that, there's probably some really weird stuff," she scoffed.

"There is, but there's also some really lovely things as well. This one says 'You're beautiful' and this one is a poem about love," I informed her.

I followed her into the room that had previously belonged to the girls but had since been emptied out. A girl everyone had spent their time making fun of sat at a table wailing while the nurse dug around the crease of her elbow with a needle. "She's really deep veined, they're having a hard time sticking her," my nurse told me when she caught me glancing over in her direction.

I sat down across the table from her and held my arm out expectantly. Instead of reaching for the bucket of needles, vials, and alcohol swabs, she reached for my arm and began to stroke it. She ran her fingers across the multitude of raised scars and asked, "Do you keloid for everything?"

"Um yeah, pretty much," I stuttered, completely taken aback.

She withdrew her hand suddenly as if she had just realized she was actually stroking a dissected eyeball, "Wait, are these self harm?"

It amazed me how little knowledge people employed in psychiatric wards seemed to possess. Time and time again they amazed me with their utter ignorance. I blushed and looked down at the ground, wishing she would just draw my blood and let me leave. "Yeah, they are," I mumbled.

The rest of our interaction was silent. She tied the tourniquet around my upper arm, felt around for a vein, and pushed the needle deep into my flesh. I had grown to love the miniscule sting and didn't flinch. I watched the maroon blood drip into the vial and slowly fill it up. The needle was removed from my arm before the small puncture wound was bandaged and I was dismissed.

I spent the remainder of the day talking to Autumn as much as possible and trying to learn how to shuffle cards. My hands were clumsy and uncoordinated as I attempted to manipulate the cards to fall into a neat stack. I spent hours completely absorbed in splitting the deck and shuffling repeatedly. I played a few games of trash, a card game that was entirely novel to me. I stared at the clock, waiting for it to alert me that it was time for bed so I could sleep off my boredom. I took some sleep medications after the veterans of the facility recommended them to me, claiming they would help. They didn't, and I still had trouble falling asleep, but I was relieved that the day had finally ended.

In the morning, I was called into the doctor's office for my daily check-in. He questioned if I was eating, I assured him that I was. It was a simple lie, but I could tell they were beginning to catch on. I reported that I was feeling great and was ready to go back to Pomegranate. He dryly suggested that I may be able to leave the following day before asking me to go get Autumn to meet with him next. Upon hearing this news and accepting it as truth, I ran to tell Autumn excitedly before sending her in.

By the time we had lined up to go to the cafeteria for lunch, the cold had become unbearable, and I asked for my pajama pants. They agreed on the condition that they removed the strings first and I gave in to the compromise and received both my pants and my hoodie, discarding the paper scrub pants for good. Some people, including Autumn, had multiple outfits to wear, I only had the clothes that had been on my back when I attempted suicide. Small pieces of toilet paper that had once wrapped pills were still in my pockets.

I gave my lunch to Autumn again, only sipping on a diet soda from the vending machine. We rode the elevator back upstairs to our unit, crowded in the tiny space by the rest of the adolescents and our nurses. The hunger was starting to catch up to me, each elevator ride left my head spinning and a dull ache spread throughout my stomach. Autumn tended to me gently, helping me off the elevators and standing behind me to catch me if I fell. When she noticed me shaking, she would ask the nurses for apple juice and bring it to me. She was so observant and patient with me, it was fate that we ended up at the same place at the same time.

I began drawing small pictures of the lighthouse painted on the wall and short poetry. A creative energy overtook me and soon I had requested more paper and begun writing entire songs about my experiences leading up to that moment. The words came to me quickly, I wrote in a frenzy churning out song after song. I wrote for hours straight, not stopping when my wrist began to cramp or my eyes became tired. The first song I wrote was entitled "A Tear in the Headlights," a play on 'a deer in the headlights.' It was about my encounter with Bronwyn in my car.

When I finished composing it, I brought Autumn to the end of the hallway and sat outside of her door while she read it. She looked up at me and loudly announced, "That's good as fuck!"

I smiled and told her the story that inspired it before sharing several other songs I had written with her. We sat there for a long time while I tested out different melodies to fit the lyrics of each song. She was so proud of me, encouraging me every step of the way and insisting I would make it big in the world. She claimed I had a talent for writing, I wasn't sure if that was true, but it certainly boosted my fragile ego. The songs were entitled, "A Tear in the Headlights," "Triage 30," "Puddle," "Phone Booth," "Therapy," "Can You See Me?" "Crimson Blood," and "Anything That Keeps You Alive." I neatly arranged the final drafts of each song in a packet I entitled "PSYCH: An Album By Faber Elliott" before requesting for it to be air stapled by the nurses.

I hid the packet in my room before it was time to go down to gym to ensure nobody would steal it or read through it without my permission. With a heart on fire for my newfound passion of songwriting, I joined the neat line of patients by the door of the unit to go downstairs. Autumn, as always, stood behind me, and excitedly rambled about my songs and how I would be famous. I was happy, but I didn't believe her. The most talented people in the world often remain hidden. After all, I was just a seventeen-year-old boy in a psychiatric ward of all places; life wasn't exactly going the way I had expected it to.

When we got down to the large gymnasium, Autumn and I claimed our usual positions in the armchairs off to the side to observe people. We recapped the events of the day and our opinions on the other patients and nurses. After a little while, my hands began to shake, and I noticed my skin had suddenly become streaked with red as if I were cold. A spinning slowly reached my head and I felt the color drain from my face.

"Hold on," I interrupted. "I think I'm about to pass out."

Autumn's face twisted into worry, "You look really pale, do you need me to get someone?"

"I don't know, I'm all shaky and I feel really lightheaded," I replied, holding up my hand to allow her to observe the tremors that had claimed it.

"I'm going to ask for some juice for you, that usually helps right?" she asked.

"That's a good idea, it's probably my blood sugar." I watched her urgently grab a nurse, pointing to me and talking quickly. The nurse walked over to me, looked me over, and instructed the other nurse to take the other patients back to the unit. She used her phone to text someone asking them to bring me juice.

Only a few minutes later, an older man appeared with two cartons of orange juice in his hands. I struggled to rip the foil covering them, so he opened them himself before allowing me to sip on them. It helped, and the feeling quickly faded. He walked me back up to the unit with our arms interlocked to have my blood pressure taken before he left.

When I rolled up my sleeves to get my blood pressure taken, a new kid walked past me and asked, "What the hell happened to you?"

I ignored him and stared at the screen, waiting for it to reveal my blood pressure. It was low, and I went to my room to lay down for a while. Autumn hadn't been in the living space, supposedly in her room as well, but I figured she would find out later that I was alright. I held my hands above my head to study my fingers, which were torn up and bloody due to me picking at them so severely. A small part of me wanted to go to sleep, but I knew that sleeping through any group therapy sessions would delay my discharge and I couldn't wait to leave the following day.

After a while, I went back to the group living area to sit through group therapy. Autumn was there and rushed up to me, explaining that she had been worried I would be taken back to the hospital and had gone to her room to block it out. She was glad I was still there and nearly hugged me before going back to her assigned seat on the other side of the room. Group therapy was boring, they talked about a helpline and passed out index cards with their phone number to put in the white cardboard boxes holding all of our documents. It was the last session of the day, and I was finally able to go to bed after it had ended.

The next morning I waited excitedly to see the doctor and finalize the discharge plans. I secretly exchanged information with Autumn, tearing the most miniscule pieces of paper up to write things down onto. Once we had written our social medias, emails, and phone numbers down, I showed her how to fold it up and where to hide it in her sock. It was a very smooth transaction, and we didn't get caught. She ran to the breakfast cart to grab food afterwards and I scribbled down a letter to Bronwyn.

The doctor called me back and I sat across from him in his office. "They say you're not eating," he claimed.

"I am!" I argued. "It's been a little harder here though, I really just need to go back to my facility. I have a lot more support there."

"Nobody has seen you eat," he replied matter-of-factly. "You're not leaving today. You aren't leaving until you earn 100 points from eating."

I felt tears collecting in my eyes, "What? That isn't fair!" Was this some sort of game to him? Why was I collecting points as if I was playing a survival game? It infuriated me beyond belief, but I forced myself to stay calm. I didn't want to be put in the so called "quiet room," the padded room I had been searched in.

"The goal is for you to learn to eat outside of your facility eventually, yes? You're going to eat here, or you aren't leaving," he concluded. "You may go now."

I jogged to my room, reaching the door just as the tears began to fall. I closed it behind me and hid behind my bed, crying. I would never eat. I would never leave. I curled up into a ball and rocked myself to self soothe. After all, nobody else was going to do it for me. I made my fingers bleed once more and sucked on the blood, letting the taste fill my mouth and ground me. I didn't cry loudly; I couldn't risk getting caught. It was a relatively silent endeavor that brought the spinning sensation back to my head.

I grabbed my packet of paper and began writing to Bronwyn, explaining why I refused to eat.

I won't eat here. I'll go until I pass out, I don't care. If you'd been in six different places since January, none of which were home, and hadn't seen your friends or gotten a hug since then, you'd want to die too. I feel like anyone would. I really hope I get out of here tomorrow. I'm honestly surprised I'm still standing. The hunger pains are intense. I just need to leave.

I was able to regain my composure as quickly as I had let it slip and soon found myself sitting next to Autumn in the living area, explaining the situation to her. I talked to a nurse about it, asking how to get 100 points. She replied that it was impossible, not a single person had ever gathered 100 points. She told me she would attempt to rectify the unfairness of the condition that had been placed in front of me. I decided to trust her and spent the rest of the day silently sulking.

When I trudged to the nurse's station in the morning to collect my hygiene items I was groggy and defeated. The moment I stood up from bed, my vision went black and I blindly stumbled through the doorway. My body was shutting down, my senses were growing dull. I showed the nurse my bracelet and she whispered, "Did you know that you're leaving today?"

Chapter Fourteen: The End of Isolation

"It's more of a relief than anything else. I'm just glad it's all over."

-Bobby Thompson

I showered and gathered my things before patiently waiting to leave. I tried to give Autumn a hug, but we were reprimanded. As a substitute, I put two of my fingers on top of hers, just as I had done with Raven before. I felt remorseful for leaving her behind, but she assured me that she would be alright and was supposed to leave the following day. We vowed to email each other and stay in contact before the nurses informed me it was time to leave. I looked back once, saving a mental image of the people and the surroundings in hopes that I would never be in a similar place again.

I was led into the lobby where I immediately spotted both Raven and Clara. I smiled and ran to join them, walking out in between them as if we were a happy family. I excitedly told them about my new friends, I hadn't seen people my age in months. I told them how wonderful it was to see and talk to people like a normal kid again, hoping they didn't take offense to the implication that I needed more than they could provide. It wasn't their fault, we would have been great friends in different circumstances, but in the current reality, even calling them friends would have prompted a reminder that they had no personal relationship with me. It was nice to feel like something other than a client, an obligation, a job, for the first time in a long time. To laugh and talk with people who weren't paid to look after me. The unspoken truth had messed with my head and amplified my loneliness.

We played the game "Which house is ours?" on the way home. It was a game I used to dread, if you didn't point out the correct house, they would drive past it for a little while and giggle at your mistake. Now I didn't mind it, the silhouette of our house had features that I could remember, and I always won the game. I recalled the first time I had played it, on my first Tuesday outing, nervously analyzing all the houses until Taylor jabbed me in the side to alert me that we were approaching the correct house to help me win. The other kids had groaned in protest, but I was grateful for the help. They had been looking forward to making fun of the new kid's mistake.

As soon as I reached the door, Cendall pulled me aside, "Faber, we want to send you to a different facility after ours. A facility specifically for self-harm and suicidal ideation, what do you think?"

"No, I don't want to go," I replied sternly. "I have to go home after this, I need to see my friends. Bronwyn is leaving for college soon and I want to do summer theatre. I told my parents I didn't want to go anywhere else after this."

She sighed, "That's what they told me, they refused unless you agreed. I know you hate surprises, so I'll be upfront with you. If you don't agree to go to another facility after this, insurance is going to cut your funds to stay here. You have about two weeks left here unless you agree to go to another facility."

"Two weeks?" I asked in disbelief. I had just tried to kill myself, I needed more than two more weeks at Pomegranate. I needed the support, the therapeutic environment, the people that had spent months caring for me. On the other hand, I was not willing to give up any more of my life to go to another facility which could be as bad as MidPoint and leave me entirely isolated.

"I'll let you know a date once I talk to insurance again," Cendall promised. She returned me to Raven and Clara before walking back to her office to make phone calls.

I couldn't believe it, I was so close to seeing my friends and leaving the people I had grown to rely on. I couldn't decipher whether I was elated or depressed, likely I felt an odd mix of both. I ate for the first time in a week at the large wooden table with Raven and Clara as music played in the background. I used my extra journal to copy down the songs I had written and begin working on new ones. I spent the entirety of my free time frantically jotting down lyrics as they came to me. My new creations didn't follow a specific theme like Psych had, they simply reflected any thought that came to me.

167

I was allowed to go on the next outing, and I chose to go to the pet store. I had convinced my parents to allow me to get a hamster when I got home, and I wanted to begin shopping for toys and treats for my new pet. Clara took me to PetLand and we were able to pet an adorable puppy during our visit. It was his first time meeting new people and at first, he laid nervously in my lap. Soon he became a bit adventurous and started licking my face and wandering towards Clara. We named the brown and white shih tzu puppy Harry, after Harry Styles. I begged Clara to adopt him, but she refused, saying she hadn't moved out of her mother's house yet. We pet and cuddled with the small dog until the staff came to take him back to his enclosure.

The following weeks passed by quickly as I prepared to go home. I had a lot of assignments to finish before my discharge and I spent a lot of my free time completing them. I wasn't able to talk to Bronwyn or Daisy on the phone to let them know I was coming home, I had to email them the good news instead. I had my graduation and received a bracelet with amazonite green and tan beads along with beads that were a mixture of grey and white. I immediately treasured it greatly. It wasn't just a bracelet, it was a symbol, and it was the last thing my favorite people in the facility had touched that belonged to me.

A new client arrived right after the conclusion of my graduation ceremony when I put two of my thumb prints on the tree in a heart shape as Taylor had done before me. Her name was Eden, and she was very quiet and reserved. I was pleased that she let me braid her hair and did it daily for my final few days. Her eating disorder behaviors were as intense as mine had been before I arrived at Pomegranate, which explained why she had gotten transferred from another facility. I didn't know her for long, but she was gentle and kind, but as terrified of eating as I had always been.

I was able to give everyone I cared about in the facility a hug before I left besides Clara and Kayleigh. I was especially disappointed at not being hugged by Clara as she had put me to bed the night before I left promising she would hug me in the morning before she went home but had gone before I woke up. I carried on the tradition started by past clients of stealing a few keepsakes, a jewel from the chandelier like Taylor and Mariana had done, and my favorite fidget toy. At last, my parents arrived and I walked out of the door with the stained glass window, never to return to my temporary home again.

After being home for a few hours, I was able to open my blue book and read the letters the staff had left me. The following letters were left for me:

Faber,

The word I am giving you is spunky.

Stay spunky my friend. I appreciate your ability to maintain a lighthearted attitude, even when times get tough. You are a funny and silly person with a lot to offer the world. Your humor can make light of things, but know that you are allowed to feel the heavy things too. When you feel those heavy things be kind to yourself! You deserve it!!

Buy me a ticket to your Broadway show? Thx!

Sincerely,

Your spunky tech Raven

Dear Faber,

You are such a brilliant human being, whose individuality shines bright. I wish you nothing but the best on your journey outside of Pomegranate. While school isn't your favorite place, keep pushing through because I have no doubt you're going to achieve amazing things.

From one Six fanatic to another, your teacher,

169

Shelby

Faber,

Good luck in all of your things in the future! Be proud of yourself and everything you have accomplished thus far. Keep trucking and never give up on yourself. I can't wait to see you make it big and famous. Keep kicking ED's ass, kid!

Kayleigh

Dear Fabes,

I wish you the best on this next adventure. Life is a rollercoaster with ups and downs. Remember to use all those skills you've learned. Don't be afraid to talk about your feelings and listen to other's feedback. Keep moving forward and stay positive. We are all going to miss you.

From,

Andrea

Hi Faber!

I give you the word: Self-Compassion.

You are so kind and thoughtful to others, but I challenge you to do this for yourself!

The world may test you sometimes, but don't let it hold you back from being the best version of yourself. Remember to challenge those automatic thoughts and leave whatever doesn't serve you behind.

This next chapter is yours to create. It can go whichever direction YOU choose. I hope nothing but happiness and good vibes for you. Now get out of your own way and allow yourself to be happy!

Always,

KV

Dear Fabes/FM/Fiber,

Thank you for being such a bright energy in the house! I never thought when I applied to this job that I would learn bad words in ASL and constantly be greeted with them. That was def not in the job description. You are such a monumental presence to know and you'll change a lot of lives one someday just by walking into theirs. Things may be overwhelming now, but you will grow, you will learn, and things will change. Heck, I'm 23 and still have the whole world waiting for me. You'll find yourself out there, please wait for him. Good things take time. Keep your friends close, but put yourself first. You deserve to be happy and free so go chase it!

Anyway, WOMP WOMP WOMP! Ya Ya Ya I am Lorde! La la la la la.

(Those were all of our inside jokes that we couldn't stop repeating for the life of us.)

Keep fighting, Faber! Reach for everything you desire. I'm rooting for you. I hope to see a Book at Barnes or hear a song on Spotify by THE Faber Elliott Laurence one day! Reach for the stars and don't stop there!

P.S. Let's pretend Harry was adopted by a really dope fam and he's doing alright!

Take care,

Your Foster Mom, Tech Clara

P.P.S. Sorry I have ugly af handwriting and ruined the aesthetic :(

P.P.S. I'm listening to Taylor while writing this and Seven literally played. What a cowinkiedink!

I nearly cried over the letters, but held it together as I excitedly held my phone in my hands for the first time in months and marveled at the little device. Home felt strange, yet there I was. I had survived the isolation.

Chapter Fifteen: A Taste of Freedom

"Freedom is the oxygen of the soul."

Moshe Dayan

When I first got home, things were perfect. I surprised my friends by showing up to their theatre performance and they both cried upon seeing me. It was less than a week before I began rehearsals for summer theatre and got to see Bronwyn five days a week. Everything was exactly how it should have been with a few changes.

I continued to struggle with self-harming and eating for months. My parents had bought a large safe to store everything sharp in and I was no longer allowed to close my bedroom door all the way. I also had weekly doctor's appointments to monitor my self-harm and my weight. At first, I didn't mind the appointments but overtime, they became more invasive and I began crying and throwing tantrums like a child to avoid going until my parents finally stopped forcing me to go.

After summer ended and Bronwyn went off to college, things went downhill for a while. I stumbled around blindly for a few weeks in her absence, contemplating suicide on more than one occasion, but eventually found my way back to Daisy. We became close again after not having talked much during the summer. Things didn't seem to stop growing darker even with Daisy by my side until one day, my parents decided to make a deal with me.

They told me that if I stopped self-harming and maintained a healthy weight, they would schedule me an appointment to go on testosterone. I agreed excitedly and held up my end of the deal and I was told that my appointment was scheduled for December 8, a day after my birthday. Unfortunately, a few weeks later, I received a call from the facility that was going to prescribe me with testosterone. They told me that my parents hadn't scheduled an appointment to go on testosterone, but rather an unnecessary therapy appointment of sorts to discuss the side effects. I became enraged, feeling I had been lied to, but my parents swore they didn't lie intentionally. Whether or not that's true may forever be debated but I personally have no reason to trust them. Luckily, because my parents had scheduled an appointment, they allowed me to schedule my own appointment with a doctor to go on testosterone even though I wasn't eighteen yet. I scheduled the appointment for December 21 and gradually found peace with waiting two additional weeks.

Today is December 7, 2023, my eighteenth birthday. To celebrate my newfound freedom of legal adulthood, I went and got a tattoo. The tattoo is on my side where I got stitches and it's of three hand drawn stars, one drawn by Taylor, one by Bronwyn, and one by Daisy. Underneath the stars it says, "You drew stars around my scars," a quote by Taylor Swift. I had first thought of the idea for the tattoo back when I was in the hospital and was more than ready to commit to it nearly a year later. Daisy went with me and held my finger nearly the whole time, only letting go to rub my elbow when it got especially painful.

To the reader, if you've made it this far: I want you to know that things truly do get better. I know that is more than cliche, but I assure you that it's true. I'm now clean from self-harm after struggling with it severely for three years. I know deep down that if I can do it, everyone else holds the same power within them. It might not get easier right away, but there will come a time when you will be at peace. If I could give one piece of advice to you, it would be to just hold on. Hold on no matter how difficult things get because you never know what could be waiting for you just around the corner. I believe in you.

Devil Child Playlist

Seven –Taylor Swift

Nothing Else Matters –Phoebe Bridgers

Gilded Lily –Cults

Je Te Laisserai Des Mots –Patrick Watson

A Sadness Runs Through Him –The Hoosiers

Matilda –Harry Styles

Funeral –Phoebe Bridgers

I Don't Like My Mind -Mitski

Caves –Gregory Alan Isakov

Paramore –Sub Urban

Mood Ring Baby –Field Medic

No Surprises –Radio Head

Fine Line –Harry Styles

Fourth of July –Sufjan Stevens

I Know You –Faye Webster

Another Love –Tom Odel

Going To Be Wonderful –Tom Rosenthal

My Love Mine All Mine –Mitski

I Know You –Faye Webster

La Petite Fille De La Mer –Vangelis

Lacy –Olivia Rodrigo

Graceland Too –Phoebe Bridgers